WE ARE
ETERNAL

WE ARE ETERNAL

WHAT THE SPIRITS TELL ME
ABOUT LIFE AFTER DEATH

ROBERT BROWN

WARNER BOOKS

An AOL Time Warner Company

Warner Books, Inc., 1271 Avenue of the Americas, New York, NY 10020
Visit our Web site at www.twbookmark.com.

An AOL Time Warner Company

Printed in the United States of America
First Printing: March 2003
10 9 8 7 6 5 4 3 2 1

ISBN: 0-446-52845-5
LCCN: 2002117221

Book design by Giorgetta Bell McRee

Thank you to all those Past and Present for showing me that it is the message, not the messenger, that is important.

Your trust in me is pivotal in educating this medium.

ACKNOWLEDGMENTS

Although so many people have been instrumental in encouraging me to write this book, I would like to specifically thank the following:

Michael, for literally living every chapter and keeping me focused.

Pam, Spirit, sent me the most amazing, organized butterfly, your belief in me has helped so many in need.

Peter Close who was the first to recognize the "diamond in the rough."

Heather and Adrian for always being there.

Carol Thomas, for her support and encouragement, also for my winter "home."

Steve and Chris Thomas of Steve Thomas BMW, thank you for your friendship and for pointing me in the right direction.

Acknowledgments

John and Sandra, for welcoming me to the East Coast and for your astute business advice.

Lilia Logette and Barbara Simons, for convincing me that I could do it and for introducing me to Lenny Rapp, my wonderful web master.

This list will never be complete without the mention of all those who help organize my tours and trips and have encouraged me in my work: Rosalind Cattanach (London), Ursula Reeg (U.S.), Martina Braunheis (Germany), Andre Studer (Switzerland), Ronnie Marmorstein (Germany), Bill and Donna Moller (U.S.), John Goldingham and Elizabeth Kennedy (New Zealand), Happy Singh (India), and *everyone* at the Learning Light Foundation (U.S.).

There are so many people around the world that have been instrumental and encouraging in gathering the information that is in this book, thank you all of you.

Last and by no means least, To Jackie Joiner, John Aherne, and Megan Rickman and all at Warner Books, thank you, we did it!

CONTENTS

Contents

Part Three

FOREWORD
BY PETER CLOSE

I feel privileged to write these few words as a foreword to my friend Robert Brown's new book. I have known Robert for more than twenty years, and during that time I have watched him progress brilliantly along the mediumistic pathway. He was a young man in his teens when I first met him, and I was immediately impressed with his ability. I persuaded him to join the Development Circle Class, of which I also was a member, and his progress was very rapid. After I left and started my own career as a medium, I convinced him to join a class that I led myself. Within eighteen months Robert was ready to start work on his own, although it was difficult at first to persuade him to make it his livelihood. Eventually he embraced his calling and soon he became extremely well known on the British circuit, and later overseas. Robert's skills have taken him all over

Europe, the U.S., Canada, India, and Australasia; and wherever he goes, his work has been praised.

Because of our friendship I have shared the platform with him on many occasions and have watched his potential expand and grow. Robert works hard to improve his craft and is never complacent. I am proud to think that I was one of his mentors, and I wish him well on this new chapter of his career.

Peter Close
International Medium

PREFACE

Since ancient times, mankind has had a fascination with what happens after our physical bodies have ceased to function. Whether we are interred in mausoleums or pyramids, buried in graves or consumed by fire, all of us hope that there is something after the efforts of this life. That our souls don't just die with our bodies. That after the pain and heartache, the joy and ecstasy, all the emotions we experience, there is some recompense or reward to be had.

Most of the world's leading religions have held out to their believers the promise of better things to come. Though most of these religions will point their followers in the general direction of what happens after they die, sadly, they are careful to prevent their followers from having complete knowledge of what is to come—perhaps out of ignorance, probably out of fear of losing control. Certainly what I have found to be true about what happens after the body dies has been known to some people for centuries. Yet it is only in recent years that there has been a definite return to thinking for ourselves, to realizing that we are responsible for the way we treat the Earth and each other and know, for ourselves, what happens to our souls. No one sect or group, individual or organization can be the sole owner of such knowledge—many have tried and failed. The truths that I discovered about life after "death" are equally available to all.

Though I'll explain my own psychic development in the first chapter, I can tell you that when I first heard of psychics and mediums who claimed to deliver messages from the so-called dead, when people told me stories of mediums in the presence of whom the dearly departed would speak, I initially dismissed such stories as complete fabrications. There was no way that these charlatans were going to fool me. These people were peddling the most evil, wicked lies ever. But no sooner did I think that than I began to wonder: What if it wasn't nonsense? What if these people were not peddling lies, but were spreading the most fantastic truth known to mankind? I was determined to find out for myself, though it was not easy for a teenage London lad to gain entrance to what appeared then the closed, secretive world of séances and mediums. Even further from my mind was the idea that I would eventually travel the world lecturing and demonstrating as a medium myself. Little did I know then that the path I followed is open to all. That all of us have the ability to understand these truths ourselves, that we don't need to rely on any one group or person to tell us what happens to our souls after our bodies pass.

I have demonstrated the gift of mediumship consistently for well over twenty years now, in many countries around the globe. It was not what I set out to do, but clearly there were other plans for me. One does not leave school and announce to the world, "I think I will talk to the dead for a living." Yet that is what, in effect, came about.

I cannot remember a time when I have been afraid of death. I have often concerned myself about the way I will die, but the actual concept of ceasing to be has never terrified me. I somehow always knew that there was more to this life.

It was during my teenage years, while others were attending dances and discos, that I started in earnest to try to understand whether there was any order to this chaos we call life, to attempt to answer that age-old question, "Is there life after so-called death?" Could it be that beyond the everyday quest to pay bills, acquire material wealth, perform the ever more difficult balancing act of living this life with all its allowed pressures, could there be a purpose? Could there be something more to life than just day-to-day living? I hope this book will help answer that question for you, in the same way that my own life experience has answered that question for me.

Mediums are rarely exciting people outside of the work they do. I myself am living proof of that fact, so I never wanted to write a book about my life, but to appreciate how I came to my conclusions it is necessary to reveal some of the path I have traveled. Though my life and my work may appear to some people as extraordinary, I'm actually not that much different from anyone else. In the same way, the people who have sought me out for consultations, be they homemakers or princesses, paupers or millionaires, have led vastly different lives, yet have many a situation in common.

I do not consider myself a great minister. I have never sought to convince or convert. My journey has, to some degree, been selfish. I wanted to know and I dared to ask.

Along the way I have been fortunate to be allowed to work with many people, whether parents coming to terms with the death of a child, or children recovering from the loss of a parent, or people recovering from involvement in suicide, murder, miscarriage, or "accident." After these past twenty-odd years I cannot think of any form of passing that I have not come into contact with. All these people have added enormously to my understanding and knowledge. For them it was an opportunity to gain some peace of mind, the chance to see if loved ones do indeed go on. For me, time and again, it has been an opportunity to test and retest the claims made by spirit communicators, that there is no death. On many occasions the sittings have proven emotional for all concerned, but to me a successful sitting occurred when information that could not have been known by anyone present was later confirmed to be true. This rules out telepathy and "cold reading," and, if the information is only checkable after the sitting, it also rules out fraud. I should also note that I vowed long ago never to reveal the contents of a sitting: They are all tape-recorded for clients. It is through the generosity of some of these clients that their experiences are told in their own words in this book. I do not believe that I the medium have any right to reveal such details.

Once we begin to understand that there is no death, that this has been proven time and again, we can start to comprehend the reason for our very being. We can stop fearing the future, begin living in the present, and begin to see the reason for the many lessons in our lives. Why do people appear to pass through our lives, when we wanted them to stay? Why do we not get everything that we think we should? Why do some things happen that just aren't fair? If we think for one moment that life does continue after so-called death, our entire perspective changes. What implications could that have for our thoughts, actions, and deeds now?

There are rules and regulations for life, but they are not man-made. They are universal laws that follow through as sure as night follows day. By understanding them and working with them, by cooperating with instead of fighting against them, we can live the lives that we desire, choose, and deserve. We can come to peace with the things that happen to us and around us. Like all great truths, these laws are very simple. Over the centuries mankind has sought to explain these laws, often complicating them in the process, through ignorance and fear of the many religious institutions, through the egos of scientists who found evidence of these laws but who could not demonstrate, within their limited comprehension, their workings. Whether you are an atheist, Jew, Muslim, Buddhist, Christian, or of any other religion or none, the laws are the same. These laws govern us all. So we have a lot more in common than some would have us believe!

It is my belief that the time has come for us all to understand these laws and take charge of our lives, for the future of all life. The continuity of our cultures, our beliefs, our planet depends on this. To do this we must obtain knowledge of the workings of these universal laws. The many roads, avenues, and blind alleys that I have traveled in pursuit of these natural laws and the answer to man's oldest question about life after death have led me to the conclusion that WE ARE ETERNAL.

The beginning of knowledge is the discovery of something we do not understand.

—FRANK HERBERT

WE ARE
ETERNAL

PART ONE

CHAPTER 1

Different Country, Same Question!

Whether I'm in New Zealand, Europe, the United States, India, or any country that I have visited, whenever it comes to the question-and-answer times after my readings, I can virtually guarantee that one of the first questions I'll be asked is, "When did you first become aware of spirit? When did you first realize that you had psychic gifts?" I can guarantee that this is the same question most mediums are asked. This question is invariably followed by, "Why you?"

Like most people, I can't remember many parts of my childhood. My family tells me that certain things happened when I was young, but I have absolutely no memory of them! But when I am asked how I first became aware of spirit, the incident is as fresh in my mind as anything that happened today or yesterday.

There were five children in my family and I was the baby. My mother had me late in life, and to have a child at almost forty years of age in the 1950s in London,

England, was quite unusual. Needless to say, I was the spoiled one, and my three sisters and brother were not pleased to have their pecking order changed by this usurper.

Our family was not rich by any stretch of the imagination; in fact, materially we were poor, but we were all very much loved. Being poor meant sharing bedrooms and wearing hand-me-down clothes, amongst other hardships. And because my mother had five children to contend with, when it came to bath night the older kids would have the actual bath, and often my mother would wash me in our old ceramic kitchen sink. I was about five years old when, one Friday evening, Mum was washing me as usual in the sink, and for some reason she was called to our front door and I was left alone, probably for no longer than five minutes. In those five minutes, though, my life was changed forever.

I was sitting in the little plastic bowl that had been placed in the sink, just splashing in the few inches of water. In front of me were the faucets, a little above them was the window, and it was dark outside. I was looking up at the window, when quite suddenly a man's face appeared; he was smiling, then laughing and pointing at me. This frightened me, and I began first to cry and then to scream. My poor mother came running and tried to calm me, and through my tears all I could say was, "The man, the man at the window was laughing at me." Before you think it was just a peeping Tom, I should mention that at the time we lived in an apartment that was five stories up, a good one hundred feet above the ground! Though my mother tried to convince me that there was no such man in the window, we had not seen the last of that visitor, for he was to return and make himself known again.

That incident in the tub is so real to me it is almost as if it was permanently etched on my memory. I cannot tell you how my sixth or seventh birthdays were celebrated. They were clearly happy times, and we have the films and photographs that show this, yet I cannot recall any specific details about them. But if you ask me about what happened on that night when I was just five years old, I can practically relive every moment of it, except that now I understand there is nothing to fear.

The second time I came across the mysterious laughing man, I was around eight years old, a shy child who did not mix very easily with other children. Although I had four siblings, I spent much of my time alone. I had a fascination with all the old family photographs and documents that Mother kept in what we called "Mum's Egyptian bag." This had been a present from my father, which he had brought back from his time in the service during World War II. It was full of birth and death certificates, obituary cards, and personal letters. Along with the photographs in Mum's precious bag there was a photograph album. My father was born in 1918 and my mother the following year, so many of the wonderful photographs and documents that had been handed down actually came from the Victorian era. And Mum kept everything. Though she could not understand my fascination with these old photographs, she was always very patient in allowing me to look through the album "one more time." Many an hour I would spend just turning the pages and looking at the pictures, mostly of people I had never met. One day I came across a photograph that had been tucked behind another. It just fell out as I turned the page, and there staring up at me was the face I had seen at the window. I cannot explain it, I just knew that I had seen him before. Instantly I had a flashback and clearly recalled sitting in the sink crying. It was like reliving the experience, except that this time I was not scared, I was curious. Who was he? I wandered into the kitchen where Mum was busy preparing dinner, "Mum, this man, do you remember I saw a man at the window? This is him." My mother glanced at the photograph, and I saw the color drain from her face. She looked ill. She took the photograph from me and told me to go back into the sitting room. After a short time Mother came to speak to me. I could see she had been crying. I was sure I was in trouble. Mum said that it was impossible for me to have seen that man and that I was not to mention it to anyone ever again. I persisted, "Mum, I did see him, I know him but don't know how or when I met him." In desperation my mother explained that the photograph was of her brother, whom she had loved very much, who had died tragically some years before. I had never met him and she told me I was not to mention seeing him ever again. "After all," she cautioned me, "they lock people up for talking like that."

No one can blame my mother for reacting the way she did. She was being confronted with something she did not and could not understand. A superstitious lady, my mother never walked under ladders, would not let a black cat cross her path, and always threw salt over her left shoulder if any was spilled in the house. Being told by your favorite child that he had seen your dead brother must have been a frightening and confusing experience for her, and yet this was not a new occurrence in our family. My brother, who is seven years older than I am, told me years later, after I had become a professional medium, that he had seen spirits as a teenager. At one point while I was growing up, several kids in our area were seeing "ghosts," and it was taken seriously enough for the local priest to come along and bless the flats where we lived. Whether these sightings were genuine or not, I cannot say. All I know is the experience I had was very real. From that point on mother never mentioned the incident again. Over the years, I did manage to get her to answer a couple of questions about this previously unknown man: "What was your brother's name?" "Ernie," was the reply. "How did he die?" "Cancer," she replied, and immediately she would get flustered and change the subject.

Apart from these two formative experiences at ages five and eight, nothing truly extraordinary happened during my childhood except that I did have this uncanny (and unnerving!) ability to know when some people would die. Though I wasn't aware of it at the time, I was able to perceive—and read—auras. Occasionally I would blurt out to my mother, "Mrs. So and So or Mr. X does not have long." My mother would be shocked and tell me that it was a wicked thing to say. I did not think it wicked myself, since I knew that *I* had nothing to do with their passing. Rather, I would just notice that the vibrant colors that I saw surrounding most people did not surround these people; the mist that floated around them was close to their bodies and a sort of brown, lifeless color. Somehow, I instinctively knew that this meant their time was up. These predictions were seldom incorrect.

I have always, even from an early age, been interested in religion—any and all religion. When my brother and sisters and I were young, my parents sent all of us to Sunday school. First, we attended Sunday school at St. Mary's Church of England in Islington, London, where I loved hearing the stories from the Bible and used to daydream a lot. Then someone discovered that the local Baptist church ran a youth club where they gave free orange juice and biscuits. Suffice it to say, we switched to that school quite quickly. But before you could have the juice you had to repeat all the prayers and lessons they taught. I remember at the age of about nine being refused the freebies by a dragon of an old lady, because I had brought along a new friend. I had told—even promised—him that we would get juice and biscuits! But when the dragon lady spoke to him and found out that he was a Catholic, she said, "We don't have those people here." Even then, I couldn't understand why some people's view of religion was so narrow: One day she told us about brotherly love, the next she refused my newfound friend. But she would not budge on the issue, and I was refused the goodies, too, being instructed to make friends only with my "own kind." We left the Baptist church but not before we kids had a great time playing in the baptismal font!

The Salvation Army was the next church to get our attention; I loved the music and my parents said that the Army did good work for many, but there were so many rules to follow! You could only marry another Salvationist, although why that bothered me at the age of ten I have no idea! It was clear that I was becoming what some termed a rebel, in the area of religion anyway!

When I was about twelve my eldest sister got married. Her husband was Jewish, and she had to convert to Judaism in order to marry him. This caused a lot of problems, as my mother refused to go to a synagogue and his mother refused to go to church. My sister and her husband compromised and got married in a civil office first, and later my sister and brother-in-law had another wedding in the synagogue.

By the age of fifteen I had seen and experienced a little bit of quite a few religions. In addition to being aware of my sister's Judaism, I had also flirted with

Buddhism in the late sixties and early seventies, thanks to a friend whose parents were complete hippies. I had learned enough to realize that there was good and bad in all of them. Each certainly had its merits, and yet each seemed to be limited by rules and prejudices.

I did not realize it at the time, but I now believe that Spirit was guiding me, giving me an immersion course on all the options open to mankind. I was not led by the nose, I simply freely followed my natural curiosity. I was looking for something more, and in sending out that thought, Spirit was soon to answer my quest.

Why me? Why was I given this psychic gift? While I believe that everyone is psychic to some degree, it is clear that some have an innate sense that can be further developed. Are mediums born with their gift? I believe they are. Just as most people can swim, though only those who practice become champions, so mediums are born, and it is up to the individual to want to develop, to dare to ask the questions that have puzzled mankind from the beginning of time. It was my good fortune to have the courage to ask those questions. Eventually, my innate psychic gifts and my curiosity about religion came together. I was sixteen when I was introduced to my good friend and mentor Peter Close, who set me on the path of self-discovery. In this way Spirit answered my request.

CHAPTER 2

Fantastic Truth or Wicked Lie?

Ask, and it shall be given you, seek, and you shall find;
Knock and it shall be opened unto you.

—MATTHEW 7:7

Peter Close is an extraordinary man. He was a friend of my family, and when I first became aware of him he had already been a serving police officer for twenty years in England, and was at that time a police sergeant. Peter had been born in the north of England. His brother, Brian, was the captain of the England cricket team. His mother, Esther (always Mrs. Close to me), was a wonderful, loving person who I soon found out was also a healer and had considerable experience with a group called Spiritualists. In 1973 my mother and I went to visit Peter at his new apartment in Kings Road, Chelsea, a very trendy area then. During this visit I listened as Peter spoke of the comfort he had found by attending meetings held by these "Spiritualists." Although I did not know the details, it seemed that Peter had gone through a very traumatic experience with a relationship, and that these Spiritualists had somehow helped him. It was to be years later that he revealed to me that he had actually come quite close to a complete breakdown.

During the course of this visit, I would glance up at Peter as he was talking and notice his eyes scanning his large sitting room, as if he were watching something that was invisible to my mother and me. After about an hour of talking, I must have become tired or bored, and my attention had wavered. Suddenly, I heard my name mentioned and just as I refocused on the conversation I saw a cat leaving the room. "I didn't know you had a cat," I said. "I love animals." Well, that was enough to send my superstitious mother off. "A cat, it's not a black cat is it? I'm not keen on cats!" she stammered. Peter made some excuse that it must have been a neighbor's cat—a nonblack one!—that had wandered in but that it had gone now. It was about a year later that Peter revealed that he had never had a cat, nor did any of the neighbors—in fact, they were not permitted to have them in their apartments. Yet, he had seen the cat as clearly as I had. We both wrote down a description of the cat as we remembered it, a year later, without ever discussing the details. The descriptions we wrote were identical.

What I did not know was that in addition to attending Spiritualist meetings, Peter had also been sitting in a development circle, to assist in the development of what he believed were his mediumistic abilities. He had been praying for a sign, any sign, that his clairvoyance was developing. He loved animals also, cats in particular. The sight of the mysterious cat that day, confirmed by someone else, who had no knowledge of such things, encouraged him enormously. I, on the other hand, despite the fact that I had confirmed someone else's clairvoyant abilities, thought all this talk about spirits and the dead communicating to be nonsense. When you are dead, you're dead, right? But the religious rebel in me was also intrigued. I was certain that if I could see one of these Spiritualist meetings, I would soon solve how they did it, how they were able to convince people that they were communicating with people who had passed. I initially thought the Spiritualists were incredibly low, that they preyed on people, gave them false hope. How mean can you get? The problem was how to get into one of these meetings. Since I was only sixteen, I asked my mother to come along with me, but, "No way," was her reply. Peter said he would take me, but only when I was a little older. Of course, the more people tried to discourage me, the more I wanted to take part, and I am sure at this time I began to see myself as some kind of potential hero. I would expose these mediums, put an end to their trickery. People would thank me for saving them from the pain of deception. All it would take would be for me to see one of these "mediums" at work and I would be able to expose them, no problem, case solved.

I found out that Peter went to his classes on a Tuesday evening at a place called the Spiritualist Association of Great Britain (SAGB), 33 Belgrave Square, London. If I described Chelsea, the area where Peter lived, as "trendy," I can only say that Belgrave Square was positively grand! A stone's throw from Buckingham Palace, in an area where many countries had their embassies, 33 Belgrave Square was a very imposing-looking building. Since Peter had denied my first request to see a medium demonstrate, I asked if I could come along one Tuesday evening and maybe just look at the books they had for sale. Perhaps I would find something that could help answer some of the questions I had. Peter agreed and said that his class would last about one and a half hours, and that I could wait by the bookstall or downstairs in the basement café for him. Most people attending the SAGB at that time congregated in the café before lectures and classes so I tagged along with Peter and his group for a cup of tea before they went off to their class.

One look around the basement café convinced me that I was right. These Spiritualist people were not only clearly mad, but their madness obviously came with age, as the average age of the thirty or so people sitting in this little café seemed to me to be about sixty-plus. They were quite a mixed bunch, milling around and chatting, and I took great delight in eavesdropping on some of their conversations, which only confirmed my instant judgment that they were all "sad, mad, and easily fooled."

"My dear," said one elderly lady with blue-rinsed hair to another very chic lady with enormous diamond earrings, "I saw Mrs. Leonard several times, quite fantastic, Oliver Lodge arranged it for me."

"Not so long ago I had a marvelous sitting with Ena Twigg," replied the diamond lady.

Other conversations flowed around me.

"Got some remarkable evidence from that American chappie, Arthur Ford, when I saw him in the fifties, told me things only I could know, military stuff, hush, hush, you know," said an elderly man, tapping his nose in a conspiratorial way. I listened to more of these conversations for about thirty minutes, and it began to dawn on me that none of these people actually appeared sad. In fact they seemed quite animated and happy. Although some seemed a little eccentric, in truth, none of them acted erratic or crazy. It was beginning to dawn on me that these people weren't fools. They spoke and conversed in an educated and intelligent way and seemed confident in the matters they discussed.

A few minutes later a man asked if he could join me at the table, and we struck up a conversation. He asked me what I was doing there. I explained that I had wanted to go to the medium's demonstration but was unable to, so I was looking for some books. He told me that he and his wife had tickets for the demonstration but that at the last minute, she had decided she did not want to go. He seemed a little unhappy, but did not reveal why he was there, only that he and his wife had had "some sadness," which he did not seem willing to discuss. He offered me his wife's ticket, but I said I could not take it, as I had to meet a friend soon at the bookstall. I did not have the courage to tell him the real reason—that I could not afford the price of the ticket! As he left, almost as an afterthought he said, "I'll tell you what, I will leave this ticket in case you change your mind. If not, see if anybody else can use it, but the demonstration starts in ten minutes. Never waste an opportunity, young man," he said as he left the café.

Well, I had desperately wanted to go to the demonstration and I was sure that I would be able to lay bare the trickery these people must employ, and here was my chance. My heart was beating as I climbed the stairs to the meeting hall. What was I doing? I did not have any idea of what even went on in these places! I would just sneak a peek at the hall where the demonstration was being held, turn around, and go home, I thought, but my feet kept heading for the meeting room. The hall was located on the first floor of the building and was named the Oliver Lodge Hall, the same name I had heard downstairs in the café. He must have been important, I thought.

When I entered the room I found that most of the seats had already been filled. Over eighty people had already been seated. It was a large double room and I was directed toward the vacant seats at the back of the hall. This was fine by me, as from that vantage point I would still be able to see all that was going on. I was also getting rather nervous about what was going to happen. Was it like the silly television shows I had seen about mediums? Would an elderly lady with a ridiculous turban and a crystal ball sit at a table and repeat, "Is anyone there?" I really had no idea what I was in for. I just knew that I would be able to see through any cheating or fraud.

The first person to stand up on the platform at the other end of the room introduced herself as the chairperson. It was, she stated, her job to introduce the medium and to assure all of us that there was nothing to be afraid of, and that should the medium address any of us we were to answer nice and clearly yes or no *only* and give no other information. Then she announced, in tones one would expect for the launching of a great cruise ship, "It is my great pleasure to introduce our medium for this evening, Mrs. Gaye Muir." I was surprised: The lady who then stood did not look strange at all. Mrs. Muir smiled at everyone and asked us to join her in prayer. After a short prayer, Gaye Muir started what she called her demonstration of clairvoyance. I do not remember all of it, but I do recall her going to several elderly ladies and telling them that their husbands or mothers were here with them. She then gave many details, names, dates, and places, to which most of the recipients eagerly nodded their heads and said "yes."

Being skeptical, if not cynical, I began to think, "Well, as most of these ladies are over seventy there is a good chance their mothers have already died, and as there seemed to be many more women present than men, surely that indicated their reason for being here—they had been widowed and were looking for some male companionship." Oh, yes, I was beginning to work it all out, pick an elderly lady, indicate that there was an older woman or a man expressing love and let the victim supply the answers to the questions. But when I listened, not just to what I wanted to hear, but *really* listened, it dawned on me that the medium only made statements, she never asked any questions. "Your husband passed with a cerebral hemorrhage?" "Yes" came the reply. "He says to tell you July." "Yes. July 18. Our wedding anniversary," was the tearful response. And so the meeting progressed. But because she was only making statements, I began then to think that all the people that the medium went to must be plants, working with the medium. If only she would give me a message, then I would know for sure. Part of me desperately wanted the medium to address me: In fact, at several points, while she was finishing one message and before she started another, I was convinced that she was going to speak to me. Each time my heart jumped, wanting her to give me a message, yet I sank further down in my chair, hoping that I would not be singled out. I actually began to sweat, out of anticipation, nervousness, perhaps fear?

All too soon the chairperson called an end to the proceedings. Gaye Muir sat down. Although I had witnessed some dozen messages, purportedly from those who had died, I had heard nothing that was going to convince me. At the same time, I hadn't heard anything to convince me that the medium was an absolute fraud, either. And then, just as the chairperson was about to ask us to join in and show our appreciation of Mrs. Muir, the medium stood up, held up her hand, and said, "I am sorry, ladies and gentlemen, I do not usually do this, but I have one brief but important message. And I want to address the young man at the back of the hall." Please, let the earth open up and make me disappear, I thought!

Gaye Muir continued to explain that she did not profess to understand what she was about to say, and hoped that if I could not accept the message that I would ask my family about it. "I have a man here, he says he is your uncle, he speaks the name Ernest or Ernie, and all he has to say is that he is sorry he scared you when you were younger. This man took himself over, you will be able to check this out, and in time help many who have had loved ones who have committed suicide. He will help you." There followed some talk about this not being the medium's "normal" kind of message, but she had to "give what she was given." The meeting closed and my head was spinning. How could she have known about my uncle? How did she know his name? How he had scared me outside the kitchen window? But she did get something wrong, I told myself. My mother had informed me that my uncle had cancer, but the medium had stated that he had committed suicide. Clearly if it really was my uncle she would not have gotten the cause of his passing wrong.

I was almost in a dream walking down the stairs, and was only brought to full consciousness by seeing Peter Close, pacing the floor waiting for me. Peter and his group wanted to know where I had been, and when I explained about the man in the cafeteria offering the ticket to the demonstration and tried to explain what had happened, they all thought we should wait and speak with this gentleman, that we would surely catch him as he made his way down the stairs and out of the building. They wanted to "thank him, et cetera," and though I wanted to thank him properly, too, it was the et cetera I was concerned about! Well, we waited until the building was clear, and though there is only one exit from 33 Belgrave Square, we never saw him leave that evening. In fact, for quite a number of years after that fateful night, I was a student and then a teacher at Belgrave Square, but I never saw that gentleman again.

Before going their different ways home, Peter and his group always used to go for a coffee and discuss what had taken place in their class that evening. This evening they invited me along, as they all wanted to know about my experience. I related everything—especially the special message at the end—and they all seemed genuinely pleased for me. I really could not see what the big deal was. After all, the medium had gotten something very wrong. My uncle had not killed himself, he had died of cancer. They all had their views about this inaccuracy. "The medium can sometimes be wrong," said one. "Perhaps she was picking up someone else's condition," said another. I was not convinced by their theories; of course I had no idea at this point what subtle vibrations mediums work with. I didn't even have a clue whether a medium could be wrong or right. All I could think of was that if it were someone who had died who was actually communicating, then surely they would not get the facts wrong. But perhaps they were right. While walking to the bus after our coffee, it was Peter who said, "Is there anyone else you can ask about this uncle?"

I had not thought to question what my mother told me about Ernie, but perhaps that's just what I needed to do. I did not want to go behind my mother's back, so on several occasions when Mum and Dad were sitting at home, I would turn the conversation around to my trip to the Spiritualist meeting. This would have my mother raising her eyes heavenward, asking no one in particular why I could not do normal things instead of wanting to "hang around" with ghost hunters! My dad, on the other hand, would often say, "Let him talk about it if he wants to." He often encouraged me to ask questions and sometimes even suggested some for me to ask my new friends. It was on one of these evenings that I mentioned what Gaye Muir had said about my uncle. I said that as the medium had obviously gotten the facts wrong, it was clearly some form of trickery and I had not found any truth in spiritualism, so perhaps it was time to find something else. The room fell silent, and before my mother could say, "Good thing too," my father quietly said, "Tell him Vi, he should know."

My mother, who had the wonderful name of Violet Phoebe D'Arcy (Vi to my father), sat at the table in our front room and told the story she had hidden for so long. Her brother, Ernest, "Ernie," as he was known, had been very successful in business, and he had managed to buy several newspaper shops. His personal life, on the other hand, had seen much sorrow. He had indeed committed suicide. Such was the shame attached to such acts in those days that my mother and indeed several other members of the family found it easier to say that he had died of cancer, rather than expose themselves to the hypocrisy of the day by revealing that he had "taken himself over." On seeing my mother's pain and yet realizing that talking about it brought some overdue relief, I decided at that point never to judge anyone who had been driven to such desperation, ever. What is more, I was determined to find out what did happen to suicides once they had passed over. I already knew what the different religions had to say about such acts—and much of it was not good. Furthermore, with my mother's confirmation of the circumstances of Ernie's death, it was clear that the medium Gaye Muir had, in fact, relayed a message that contained information, facts that did not—and could not—come from me. Gaye Muir had indeed had contact with my uncle Ernie. I had to find out more. Was this a fantastic truth?

Where do you start, to whom do you turn when you think you know what you want to do, but have no idea how to go about it? I was desperate to find out more information about Gaye Muir and her mediumship abilities, but my parents were justifiably concerned—after all, I was only sixteen! But as both my parents knew and trusted Peter Close, they turned to him for advice and guidance. Peter somehow assured them that I would be all right, that the Spiritualists were good people who were not trying to trick or brainwash anyone. He also thought that it would be a good idea for me to meet Gaye Muir. He knew that she ran a development circle and as a teaching medium she might be able to give me the guidance I needed or at least answer some of my questions. He arranged for me to have a meeting with Mrs. Muir the following week.

CHAPTER 3

Open My Eyes

When the student is ready, the teacher will appear.

—BUDDHA

My first meeting with Gaye Muir was really a joy. For once I had found someone who appeared to understand the things I had experienced. Without even speaking she conveyed the reassurance of someone who had witnessed similar happenings. I found it very easy to tell her of my earlier experiences, and she seemed genuinely surprised when I explained how I had attended my first meeting, and even more surprised when I told her that she had given me such important information. Gaye thought for a while about what I had told her about my surprise and about my uncle Ernie. It appeared as though she was thinking things through or mentally talking to herself. Eventually she said, "You can join our class if you like, you have the potential to be a big noise in Spiritualism and a good worker for Spirit, come along next week at 7:30 P.M." I couldn't believe what she had told me. Me? A big noise in Spiritualism? Even though I had originally gone to the first meeting to discount everything that she had said? I had no idea what to expect from this class; I only wanted to find out if it were true that people who died continued to live in some way, that indeed they did communicate. And of course, once I answered that question, another hundred questions suddenly came up. After all, what happens when we die is one of the age-old questions that everybody asks! It appeared that the only way to start to comprehend any of this was to go along to what Gaye Muir described as "our development class." The following week I turned up at 33 Belgrave Square ready to witness the great revelation: I assumed you went to one class and found all the answers, that after one hour in a class, I would have every question I ever had about life, death, and the other side answered completely. I am glad that from this point I can laugh at my own naïveté! What I did not know at the time of attending her class, and did not see any sign of during the many months I spent with Gaye Muir, was that she is known as "a tough cookie." In her own mediumship, she is determined, demanding, unstinting in her discipline and criticism of herself. What I witnessed as a student was a person of compassion and love, and certainly, in my case, a teacher of great patience. I must have driven her mad with all the questions that had been stored up for so long. I never once saw her angry, annoyed, or despondent with our efforts. Two words sum up those classes for me: gentleness and patience.

Development classes differ from teacher to teacher, I was later to find, but the weekly routine that was to become mine generally is one that is adopted by most teachers for psychic and mediumship development. The teacher sets the day and time, and rarely, if ever, is this changed. The student has to turn up at the agreed time and be willing to learn. I was willing, so much so that for the first class I was over an hour early!

When I first entered the development circle, I had no idea what to expect or what was expected of me; not a clue whether it would be held in the dark, whether I would see or hear anything, whether I was going to be scared or be able to prevent myself from bursting out in laughter. The only thing I did know was that I just had to try it.

I was introduced to the rest of the group, and we were about twelve people in all. Only first names were used. On entering the room, we were all asked to place a personal item—keys, comb, watch, and so forth—on a tray covered with a cloth. I noticed that the chairs were formed in a circle. Everyone seemed to know their own place, and I was asked to sit directly opposite Gaye Muir. The lights were dimmed, but there was still enough light for me to see everyone's features. Our teacher started by explaining what was going to happen that evening, that we would first link in a prayer for guidance and protection; we would then follow a guided meditation, after which we would attempt some psychic exercise called psychometry.

The first thing I was aware of right before we began the prayer was the silence. Here we sat in the middle of London, in one of the busiest parts of the world, yet all was quiet. I was unaware of any noise either within the room or from outside. With our prayer said, we entered the meditation period. I remember something being said about different colors, after that the next thing I heard was Gaye saying, "Now back you come, back to join our circle, back you come." I felt like such a fool—apparently I had felt so relaxed I nodded off! But no one seemed to mind. "Maybe they were being kind," I thought.

As the lights were turned up slightly, one person at a time was asked to take an article from the tray: We were not allowed to look at the article, just to put our hands under the cloth and take the first article we touched. We were then to speak of any "impressions" we felt we had from the article. The owner of the article was not allowed to comment until whoever was holding the article had finished giving impressions. The first person to pick up an object started by talking of "someone being honest, loving, very loyal, and a good organizer," and other comments in this vein. At the end the "reader" would hold the article up high and say "Who does this belong to?" Then the owner had to confirm which, if any, of the impressions were correct.

When it came to my turn, I grabbed somebody's watch. I had absolutely no idea what to say. I immediately just felt sick to my stomach that everyone else had these wonderful feelings and I felt no such thing. Eventually Gaye asked me what I was feeling. "Nothing," I replied.

"You must feel something?"

"Well, I just feel sick in my stomach, and I suppose it's because I am nervous, and probably it is because I can't do this, and . . ." A lady raised her hand. "That's my watch you are holding, and as everyone else here but you knows, I had an operation two weeks ago and it is still healing, and it was on my stomach." I really could not accept that I had gotten something—that I was able to have and communicate such an accurate impression. Perhaps I was imagining it? Maybe the lady was being kind? It troubled me. Our teacher seemed to sense this. She asked the whole class, "Does anyone else here have a stomach problem?" "No," was the answer. Almost immediately after I handed the watch back to its owner, the sick feeling just disappeared. It was explained to me that many people had lost the ability to trust their own feelings, and that what I experienced my first night in the class was a big lesson for my future development as a medium—and as a human being. Don't try to put your own interpretation on things, don't try to overthink or rationalize or doubt yourself. Simply trust and give out what you are given. This was advice I was to hear time and again over the next twenty-odd years, especially from that inimitable medium called "Battling" Bertha Harris, who often would say, "I gives it as I gets it!"

Before the class came to an end one or two people were allowed to stand up and attempt spirit communication. It was explained that these were advanced students and that the rest of us were to concentrate on sending power to them, as one day that could be us standing there. We could send power by visualizing a white light leaving our solar plexus and sending it toward the person attempting communication. I was not the recipient of any messages that night, but the ones that did get some evidence seemed pleased, and certainly the advanced students taking part seemed pleased with themselves. All too soon it was time to finish our circle. A prayer was said, and we were instructed to "close down," using colors again. Funny, I did not recall "opening up"! As we left our class, I found myself walking down the stairs chatting to one of the "advanced students." I asked how many weeks it had taken her to be able to get spirit communication. She revealed that although she felt she was making great progress in this group, she had been sitting in various development circles for seven years!

The following week I had to confide in Gaye Muir that I could not envisage attending a class for seven years or more. When you are a teenager seven weeks— let alone seven years—is a lifetime! Gaye explained that we all develop at different rates, and she felt that although I was what she termed "a diamond in the rough," if I persevered I could well see some results soon, much sooner than seven years. She asked me to give it six months, nine months tops. Her words gave me hope and confidence in my abilities, so I agreed. Gaye also explained that the decision had to be mine and mine alone, that there would always be someone to help and guide me, but that I had a "personal responsibility" for whether I would continue to develop—ultimately, the decision was in my hands only. Gaye Muir also felt that the time would come when I would need a different teacher, and that one day I would walk away from Spiritualism and then return.

The idea that I would leave Spiritualism—let alone Mrs. Muir—struck me as ridiculous. Nothing seemed further from my mind, and for the next eight months I duly turned up each week and did my best to practice meditation, psychometry, auric reading, and spirit communication. I asked as many questions as time allowed and would often leave the fantastic Belgrave Square library with three or four books at a time, such was my eagerness to learn.

Just over eight months after I had joined the development circle Gaye announced that the circle would have to be suspended for a while as she had to travel abroad to lecture. I was devastated. How could Spirit, who I now believed led me everywhere, lead me to this class only to bring me to a dead end? I was also annoyed with Gaye—how could she possibly leave me when I was just getting started? Of course, when one is a student one never thinks that sometimes the teacher has other things to do for his or her own advancement. I never returned to Gaye's classes, and in fact I am not sure if the same group ever got together again. I do know that Gaye went on to become a respected teacher throughout Europe and a very well-known medium in her own right. Although we have only met once since then, at the Psychic News dinner dance in the late 1970s, our paths have crossed several times. On my many visits to Munich, Germany, during 1998 and 2001, I met many people who had consulted Gaye. In fact, my hostess on all those occasions, Frau Ronnie Marmorstein, was happy to tell me one day that the room I used for seeing people was the same room Gaye used on her many visits. As you might imagine, I am not a believer in coincidences—I am sure Spirit brought our paths together on all of these occasions.

After Gaye left, I tried my hardest to join Ivy Northage at her "School of Mediumship," which was also, at the time, located at Belgrave Square. Ivy was considered one of the best teachers England had ever produced. She was not only a teacher but also a very well-respected medium in demand for both mental mediumship and trance work.

Ivy was definitely a "tough cookie," especially when she was teaching class. So when she heard that I was still a teenager she would not even consent to see me, but luckily, I had friends! Peter Close attended her class and was—coincidentally—one of her star pupils! After Peter had spoken on my behalf, Ivy agreed to interview me. Of course, she made it clear that there were no guarantees, that in fact she really saw no point in meeting me, and at best, all she might suggest was that I should attend a beginners class. She also told Peter that she hoped that I had some answers for the questions she intended to ask me.

To say that I was nervous and intimidated beyond belief would be putting it mildly. I spent the whole week before the "interview" cramming up on Spiritualism, the history, who was who, how modern-day Spiritualism had come about. There were very few facts that I did not know about Hydesville, the Fox family, Conan Doyle, and other well-known Spiritualist people, places, or things. I hoped that all of the information I knew might show her that my interest in developing my mediumistic gifts was genuine. Finally, the big day came and I was asked to meet Mrs. Northage in the Oliver Lodge room—there was that name again. I walked in with much trepidation. Sitting down in a simple chair at the side of the room was an immaculately dressed lady with not a hair out of place. I was first struck by how physically small she was, particularly since she had such a formidable reputation. I was even more surprised when she stood up and did not appear to grow much larger. I am only five foot seven, but I towered over the standing Mrs. Ivy Northage. I was more than ready for my interview. "Bring on the questions, little lady," I thought to myself, "I have memorized all the answers!"

Ivy Northage looked at me and said, "Now then, I have but one question for you, young man. Why do you want to develop mediumship?"

I was stunned! No one had prepared me for this. I was sure she was going to ask me what I had done, what had I learned. I stuttered. I began to panic. What should I say to this most unexpected question? I had originally become interested in Spiritualism as almost an academic exercise—I wanted to prove that they were phonies and were only trying to trick people. But I had studied for months with Mrs. Muir, I had read much and seen and heard things I never would have thought possible. Why *did* I want to develop my abilities? I distinctly remember thinking to myself in that moment of silence, "If anyone is there, please give me an answer. Please help me." Without being fully aware of it, I found my mouth moving and heard myself say, "Because I want to help other people, Mrs. Northage."

Ivy Northage continued to look at me. At last, she spoke. "Good," replied Ivy. "If you had said anything else, you would be walking out of that door now. As it is, I will tell you the rules of our circle and you may join us, in the beginners group."

It was then that I knew I was going to be a medium for the rest of my life.

It is an interesting point, but all the great teachers I have met always refer to the development groups as "*our* circles," never "mine" or "theirs." Below are Ivy's rules, which she outlined for me on that day and which I was expected to follow at all times:

1. Do not turn up for circle late, out of respect for Spirit and your colleagues.
2. Should you be late, do not attempt to join the circle once it has started and the door is closed.
3. You may miss one meeting every twelve weeks, if you have a very good reason. If you miss twice, don't come back.

These were the basic rules for attending the Ivy Northage School of Mediumship. But when it came to discipline within the circle, there were even more rules. Ivy explained that as she was busy with the advanced circle I would be joining a group run by her assistant, who at that time was Win Kent. There was quite a set procedure for these circles: First there would be prayer, followed by the opening of the chakras, or psychic centers. After a meditation, we would engage in psychic exercises such as psychometry (the reading of inanimate objects) or flower clairsentience, where someone would bring a flower, and without knowing who was the owner, we would "read the flower." Reading flowers worked on a subtler vibration than psychometry, as flowers, it was explained, are living things and therefore work on higher vibrations than nonliving objects. You could find out more about people, what they are really like, by reading the living flowers they brought in than you could from personal items, which might have been someone else's or might have old or past conditions attached to them. I was also learning a lot about vibrations and was being introduced to the different forms of mediumship, something I had not considered before.

One very important aspect of this school was that Ivy insisted that those being groomed to work as mediums should be given the opportunity to experience working in front of an audience or congregation. Every three months or so a meeting would be held where the general public would be invited to attend and we would have to do our best at spirit communication. There were, of course, rules for this too!

We weren't able to use or introduce our guides (I'll explain the purpose of a guide a little later on). The idea was that a public demonstration was to *prove* the continuance of life. Trying to get people unschooled in the ways of mediumship or skeptical of the other side to accept the idea that they were accompanied by some helper or guide they had never known would be asking too much, particularly since many guides were Tibetan, Chinese, or Native American! Forcing people to accept something so foreign to them would more than likely turn people away from Spiritualism, rather than toward it, so we were to avoid any discussion of guides altogether. Rather, our directions were:

1. We were to link with someone in spirit whom someone in the audience had known.
2. We were to give factual evidence to the person that spirit had directed us to ("the sitter"). The sitter could only answer Yes or No to our statements. We could give physical descriptions or names and provide details about the relationship between the sitter and the spirit—all of these were acceptable.
3. No questions were to be asked of the sitter.
4. If the sitter could positively agree that he or she knew who the communicator was, then, and only then, we could give a small message to the sitter.

The reason for our demonstration was to prove life after death to the audience and to discipline us. Many mediums fail because they believe delivering a message from the communicator to the sitter is the most important part of a sitting. Delivering such a message will make the medium appear particularly gifted, and very powerful. However, the important part is actually simply proving the continuance of life after death, making the sitter believe that our souls don't die with our physical bodies. Mrs. Northage did not believe in egos and made us believe—and rightly so—that as mediums we were but small cogs in the whole works.

After about a year of sitting in this beginner's class, I was told that at the next public meeting I would be joining the advanced students, for one evening only.

Mrs. Northage herself would be chairing this demonstration, and it was well known that she could and would step in at any point she deemed fit and correct any mistakes that she felt were being made by the students. These evenings were, to put it mildly, nerve-racking for all the participants. There were six of us giving readings that evening and we were expected not only to convey information, but also to speak clearly, not ask questions, and, on top of everything else, look good while doing it! It was to be many years later, working with my good friend John Edward, that I was finally persuaded to appear on a platform without a tie, such was the impact of Ivy's method of teaching and the standards she demanded. I watched as one by one the five people before me were criticized, chided, advised, and helped by Ivy Northage. Then it was my turn. I remember it well. I stood up, smiled at the fifty or so people in front of me, and then glanced at my five colleagues alongside me. They all beamed back, one surreptitiously giving me the thumbs-up sign. Thank goodness Ivy missed that! I pointed to a middle-aged lady in the front row. "I am linking with you," I said. Up jumped Ivy Northage. "Why are you going to this lady?"

"Because I am being told to," I said.

"Then state, 'I am being told to come to you.'"

"I am told to come to you," I said to the woman. "Is your husband in spirit?"

"Are you asking this lady or telling her? Why do you think it is her husband?"

"Because I saw a man," I replied, "and he said, 'say husband.'"

"Then give what you get, say, 'I have your husband here.'"

By now I was beginning to get annoyed and frustrated with Ivy's interfering. I was unaware at the time that Ivy had the ability to follow the whole process of these messages—she could see and hear exactly what I was seeing and hearing as I linked with the woman in the front row. I was to watch her many times later, cajoling, teaching, and guiding students. It was uncanny. Right before her students provided some evidence or pertinent information, she would say, "That's it, you've got it," and listen as her students provided proof. Similarly, Ivy was also aware of my frustration and she changed tack.

"Okay, you said you saw the man? Then you should be able to describe him!"

I began to describe the man I saw. "He had dark hair, round face, looked about as tall as me."

"Yes, that sounds right, " said the sitter.

"Not enough detail, ask him for something specific!" Ivy suddenly announced.

"Now he is holding up his hand."

Ivy pushed me forward. "Why?"

"I don't know."

"Look again, there must be a reason."

I looked at the spirit before me for what was probably thirty seconds but seemed like forever, and then suddenly I saw. "I see him holding up his hand, but indicating his index finger, he has the top of his index finger missing!"

My sitter gasped. "Yes!"

"It was his right hand."

"Yes!"

I was on a roll now. "Now I feel pains in my chest, everything seems to happen fast, I feel like I am falling down, I hear the name Dick, or Rick?"

Ivy interrupted once again. "Okay, stop there," she said. "That was good, have a seat."

As I took my seat, the sitter began speaking. "I would like to explain, Mrs. Northage. My husband, Richard, passed quickly while at work. He was an engineer and did lose a finger when he was an apprentice, the very finger this young man mentioned. He passed when he had a massive heart attack. His heart stopped beating and he just fell down."

At first I thought the whole audience were going to burst into applause, but one wave from Ivy's hand and everyone settled down. A prayer was quickly said and the meeting concluded. I was still stunned by my success—my mind was reeling. Surely this was one of the best readings Ivy had ever heard. Surely I was her new star pupil. I was positive that Ivy Northage was going to say something to me, words of encouragement, congratulations, support. I hung around until almost everyone else had left. As Ivy passed me she simply said, "Not bad."

It was my good fortune to stay in this circle, and I remained for almost eighteen months under the tutelage of Win Kent. Win was a wonderful teacher, excellent at color and its therapeutic possibilities. I learned much from Ivy, Gaye, and Win, and will forever be grateful for their kindness, patience, guidance, and willingness to share their knowledge.

One other aspect of Ivy's teaching that stood out was that she was one of the first teachers to insist that her students work in public to gain experience. We were not allowed to charge for our services. We were expected to demonstrate purely to gain experience. Peter Close, who by this time had graduated from Ivy's school, was already working in Spiritualist churches. At that time he worked with a friend named Joan. One of them would give an inspirational talk while one would demonstrate clairvoyance. The following week they would swap duties—this way they were able to concentrate on one thing at a time. I went along to as many of their meetings as I could. Soon I was to join Peter on the platform, and when he decided to form his own development circle at his home, I was one of the first to join. In time, Peter began traveling, and in his absence, I would run the circle, for him. Peter was justifiably proud of this circle since several mediums who are still working today started their development in that circle. Part of the development process in this circle was that the whole circle would go to a church and demonstrate their abilities. It was through Peter, and these demonstrations he organized, that I was eventually asked to give a solo demonstration of an evening of clairvoyance. It was to be held at the London Spiritual Mission, and I was just twenty-one years of age at the time.

That solo reading at the London Spiritual Mission was a real turning point in my professional career. From that springboard, I began giving more and more solo demonstrations, which have taught me more about life on this side and on the other side than anything else. I came to understand much about life—why people are the way they are, what is and what is not possible when it comes to mediumship, what to look for in the different forms of mediumship, what true healing is and how it works. Because of these wonderful early experiences, I went on to teach about Spiritualism, to demonstrate and advocate spirit communication around the world—which is something I still continue to do. I even went back to Belgrave Square—this time to teach—and I ran a development group for those under thirty years of age. I was to work in many Spiritualist churches throughout England over a ten-year period and was really building an excellent reputation for myself.

Then the second Gaye Muir prediction came true. I completely walked away from Spiritualism, disillusioned.

PART TWO

CHAPTER 4

Finding the Truth

Beloved, believe not every spirit,
But test the spirits whether they are of God,
Because many false prophets have gone out into the world.
—I JOHN 4:1

One of the hardest lessons I had to learn was that not everyone who claims to be a spiritualist is necessarily also spiritual. This accusation of course can be leveled at any religion, group, or organization. The world has seen more than enough of errant ministers, wicked priests, and evil mullahs. Not to mention mediums with enormous egos! This was my first disappointment.

I truly—if naïvely—believed that these mediums, who claimed to have such wonderful knowledge that "we do not die," would surely put aside their own interests and unite for the good of mankind. When one person has access to the proof of such wonderful knowledge as that, how can he or she not want to sing it from the rooftops and spread the message for the good of everyone?

My rude awakening came from a well-known medium in London. I was twenty-six years old and at the time I did not charge for my services. I had no financial need to, and from my first teachings in mediumship I had been led to believe that this was a God-given gift that did not belong to me, and therefore it was not mine to sell. I well recall getting into almost a shouting match with this medium. I can still hear her words. "By not charging, you are stealing the bread from other mediums' mouths; of course people will flock to you if you do not charge, but what about the poor mediums who have to make their living seeing people professionally?" I was stunned! I walked away, no, crawled away, absolutely shattered. Was this what it was all about? Money? If that were the case, I was going to have nothing to do with Spiritualism or mediumship at all. I had resolved to turn my back on that community entirely.

While I was licking my wounds, staying at a small house in Spain, I did a lot of reflecting and slowly began to think differently about my abilities and future as a medium. Surely to do this work well would take all my time, it would have to be a lifetime commitment. I, of course, had to live and had bills to pay. I also saw no reason for my living in a cave and begging—after all surely Spirit knew that this would make me very unhappy and consequently would affect any work I tried to do. Perhaps the medium was right. Perhaps in order to fully develop my abilities and powers, I would have devote everything I had to Spirit.

I started to revive my contacts and planned to give classes and demonstrations, only this time I would devote all my time, and therefore, it would also become my main source of income. Adopting this route would also allow me to investigate as many mediums and their abilities as I could come into contact with. I would have more free time and energy to devote to examining other mediums and their techniques. And although I did not realize it at the time, it would allow me to witness some things that thousands of people have spent their lifetime praying for.

The medium who had made me reconsider everything I thought about spiritualism and mediumship was, as it happened, the former wife of one of England's best-loved comics, Kenny Everett. Lee Everett did me a great favor when she argued with me about my approach to mediumship. Whether it was her intention or not, from that point I decided to be nothing but professional in every aspect of my investigation of and involvement in all things psychic.

On Valentine's Day 1985 Lee was married at my local Spiritualist church and I was invited. It was, to say the least, an unconventional wedding. The bride arrived holding her beloved chihuahua, the reception was held at a fish and chip restaurant, and the guest of honor was Elton John. I was recently in Geales, the restaurant in London's Notting Hill Gate, and the photographs of Elton (with me beside him!) are still hanging on the wall. So, on reflection, even those who do not initially appear to act with the most altruistic of motives can be and are used by spirit. I often wonder whether, without that hiatus, I would have gone on to travel the world as a medium.

I had witnessed mental mediumship, clairvoyance, and clairaudience, and will discuss these in detail later. My goal from the time I was around twenty was to see mediumship in all its forms, to see everything that the Spiritualist world had to offer. After all, seeing is believing, right?

In 1978 at the London Spiritualist Mission, the church where I had conducted my first solo service, I heard about an extraordinary man. Many people revered him; it was said that in his presence the dead spoke and that *all* present heard the voices of the dearly departed. His name was Leslie Flint. I was of course intrigued, but like most people—and, in fact, like many mediums—was highly skeptical of such outrageous claims. After all, surely such ability, if genuine, would be known to all. Surely it could be proven under test conditions. What I did not know was that was exactly what Leslie Flint had allowed to happen. In one famous case, he allowed himself to be tied up and gagged and asked to retain a measured amount of colored water in his taped mouth to prevent ventriloquism. He was also expected to return the same amount of fluid to a jar. There was no way he could be throwing his voice, no way that he could control anything that was in the room at the time. Still, the voices of the dead were heard by everyone present. Leslie was one of the most tested mediums ever, and yet when scientists could find no cheating or explanations (according to their limited criteria, that all things must be complicated and we need an involved explanation from one of them, which usually explains little!), they decided that they would err on the side of caution and really did not publish their findings satisfactorily, even though the truth of Leslie's abilities—and the truth about life after death—was staring them right in the face. A great gift to mankind was denied the public at that time, but thankfully, under the guidance of the Reverend Larry Taylor, the Leslie Flint Educational Trust has recently been formed and many of the taped séances are now available to those wishing to examine and learn the messages Spirit has for us. It is difficult though for someone to just accept a tape-recording, so below is my actual experience witnessing the direct voice phenomenon of Leslie Flint.

By the time I met Leslie he had already been a medium for some fifty years. He had enjoyed a great life, filling halls in his earlier days with hundreds of people from around the world who sought his services. He had given séances for many well-known people, including the actress Mae West, who was a personal friend. (For a full account of his remarkable life do read his biography, *Voices in the Dark*.)

Of course I wanted nothing more than to witness this phenomenon, and again, in my naïveté, I assumed that one just booked and went along. When I first mentioned that I wanted to attend a Leslie Flint séance to other members of the London Spiritualist Mission, they all but laughed at me. Did I not know that there were huge waiting lists? People had waited years to get an appointment; after all, many of the crowned heads of Europe were regular clients. My response then, as it still is now, was, "Oh, so if you are really seeking, sincerely want to get at the truth, you have to be someone or be rich to get to see these 'great' mediums?" Suffice it to say, the answer should be no.

One week later I got a call from Rosalind Cattanach. Ros was the secretary of the London Spiritual Mission, and, in fact, over twenty-five years later she is still the booking secretary for that much-loved church.

"Robert, were you serious when you said that you wanted to go to a Leslie Flint séance?" she asked. "I've just had two cancellations, and you are more than welcome to attend if you like." Was I serious about attending a Leslie Flint séance? I could not believe it. What's more, I assured Ros that the other ticket would be gratefully taken by Peter Close. There was no need to ask him; I assumed—quite correctly—that given the chance, everyone would want to go to such an event.

So on the appointed day Peter and I went to Leslie's home in London. It was an imposing house and we entered via the garden. The room in which the séance was held was rather featureless. I do remember Leslie pointing out a shirt that was in a glass cabinet. He explained that it had belonged to Rudolf Valentino, the great silent movie star. Leslie had long maintained that he had for many years been in contact with the late actor. As a rather interesting aside, Gwen Vaughan, one of Leslie's closest friends, cannot recall this item. She doesn't remember it ever being in the room. I have met her on various occasions since and Gwen is the guardian of most of the Leslie Flint tapes. Though she cannot recall the shirt, I know that it was pointed out to me, and I have often wondered what happened to the shirt that was once worn by the great "sheik."

The room we entered was well-lit and chairs were placed in a semicircle; there was an ordinary chair placed in front where Leslie was to sit. It was explained that the room would be locked and that no one would be able to leave until the séance had concluded. The séance was to be conducted in complete darkness. Most of the people present had been visitors before, and I think I was the only one who was a first-timer. As the lights were first lowered, then switched off, Leslie continued to encourage us to talk and then asked us to sing. The song was some World War II ditty that everyone knew and could join in. To be in a pitch-black room with a group of strangers singing is not everyone's ideal way to spend a few hours, and I began to regret attending. I then heard labored breathing and assumed that Leslie was going into some sort of trance; suddenly the room went very cold and Leslie began speaking quite consciously. This was quite fascinating, because contrary to all that I had read about other mediums who had fallen into a trance and had voices emanating from around them, Leslie Flint, at the séance I attended, was always wide awake. Often he would converse with the spirit communicators. Sometimes there was more than one voice speaking simultaneously—this alone should have knocked the theory of ventriloquism. Try getting even the most accomplished performer of that art to create three or more voices at the same time. It is impossible, I am told.

The first voice I heard after Leslie had asked if there were any messages to be conveyed was the inimitable voice of Mickey, the Cockney guide so long associated with Leslie Flint. A most convincing aspect was, not only the content of what was said, but also the fact that the voices clearly and definitely "moved" about the room. One moment a voice appeared to be addressing a person across from me, the next minute the voice was right in front of me. When the spirit guide called Mickey addressed me I was told, "He is all right, this Robert, there are people over here who think that one day he will help many people on your side of life, they think he has great potential, he will take this knowledge around the world, they promise this is possible." I was not impressed. Surely, I thought, if Spirit made an effort to actually speak and not go through another medium, it would have something more to say than words that were designed to stroke egos. If I was less than satisfied at the outcome of the séance, Peter Close was livid. When we attended that first séance, Peter was near retirement from the police force, and yet the message for him was, "People over here are talking about that Peter getting a big promotion, he is going to go a long way." Various other voices were heard; clearly some people present were very touched to hear their own loved ones' voices, and the range of the voices was impressive. As we left we discussed the day's events. Peter thought the voices were genuine, but that somehow Leslie's mind interfered with the information coming through. Peter has always looked younger than he is. Even today when people see Peter, a man now in his seventies, many think he is only in his fifties: Imagine how he looked over twenty years ago. Peter believed that the voices were from Spirit, but that on seeing him, Leslie had thought him younger than his years and somehow influenced the voices. Not long after this séance, Peter retired after thirty years in the police force. Soon after this he was working full-time as a medium; it has been a running "discussion" between Peter and me. Peter remains open-minded about the voices. I venture that from Spirit's point of view, it was indeed promotion, and he has gone a long way. For many years Peter was one of the few British mediums to be invited to America on a regular basis. At this time of writing Peter is also bringing to fruition plans he has to start work in his semiretirement, helping people in Thailand by starting a development circle. From Spirit's perception that is promotion, and he has gone a long way.

One of the important aspects of spirit communication that I learned from this was perception. It is important that we do not try to witness what we want to see or hear but try to be open-minded enough to analyze and accept the possibility that we are witnessing another mind's view—Peter Close's "promotion" is just one example of this. In order to fully understand and comprehend what is being said, we may have to change our way of thinking and accept Spirit's view of a situation, which may not be cluttered with material concerns.

I was fortunate to attend several other Leslie Flint séances, and I have to say they were extraordinary. Some of the information that came through did seem trivial, but then, how much of our lives is made up of trivial things? If a husband or loved one came through suddenly expanding on Einstein's theory of relativity, when while on earth they had no knowledge of such things, would we really believe that it was the person we knew, had they really acquired such knowledge just by the act of dying? I believed then, as I do now, that the acid test for any spirit communication is the information that comes through. Some of the séances I witnessed at Leslie Flint's undoubtedly passed that test. The information that was given through the medium Leslie Flint was and is a great benefit to mankind. I urge anyone who wonders what Spirit makes of such issues as capital punishment, vivisection, and man's inhumanity to man to listen to the many tapes that are available of the Leslie Flint séances.

Leslie Flint, one of the greatest men of spiritualism, passed to Spirit in 1994. He never claimed to know exactly how his mediumship worked. He knew some of the technicalities that had been explained to him during the séances by Spirit, but he could never answer the question, "Why him?" For some time it was thought that this form of mediumship was unique, but before and since Leslie there have been mediums in whose presence the dead have allegedly spoken. None, however, have been tested to the same degree as Leslie, although the tests currently being carried out by Dr. Gary Schwarz in Arizona are showing encouraging results with the mediums who are willing to be tested.

I have always believed that having agreed on the path of mediumship, we are after all none of us slaves, and the development of psychic ability and gifts is controlled by what the mediums can show that they are worthy of. Clearly Spirit needs to trust whomever it is working with and vice versa. I have witnessed alleged direct voice on about six other occasions, four of which were plainly bogus, but in November 1999, I attended a séance held by a well-known English medium called Colin Fry. To some people Colin is controversial. He has been criticized harshly in the press for the way some of his séances were conducted. As is the case with most mediums in the public eye, fraud and trickery

have been alleged. Yet I have witnessed him demonstrate clairvoyance, trance, and psychic mediumship.
He is a sincere and gifted human being. I hope that his
new television show in England will develop in such a
way that we will be able to witness an actual séance
with physical phenomena involved. Such a thing is
possible these days with infrared cameras and night
vision sights. Colin is one of the rare mediums who can
actually do this. Though I went to this séance with an
open mind, I made certain that he did not know my
name. In fact we had never met. He did not know who
was even arriving with the person who organized our
visit. Near the end of this séance, the unmistakable
voice of Leslie Flint filled the room. I will not reveal all
that was said but am happy to confirm that the voice
repeated word for word the same promise made by
Mickey over twenty years earlier. What I thought at
the time was a trite and trivial thing for Spirit to tell me
turned out to be an extremely powerful moment for
me two decades later. There are only two people in
the whole world who would know what had been
promised by Spirit all those years ago, myself and Peter
Close. Peter had no idea that I was going to a Colin Fry
séance. In fact he was thousands of miles away in Thailand. Stranger still, what no one but I knew was that for
the past few years, clients had been having sittings
with me that have always been tape-recorded, and they
had been contacting me after the event asking what
the other voices on the tape were. At first, I thought

this was some kind of joke or recording problem, but last year in New York, sitting with a client, we both heard a sound that was captured on tape. Could it have been direct voice communication by Spirit? By no stretch of the imagination is this form of my mediumship developed yet, but I know that direct voice communication is possible, and once we get over the preoccupation with mental mediumship we will hear more of it. In the séance at Colin Fry's home, Leslie from Spirit urged me to continue my psychic development, yet no one knew I had had this phenomenon.

I have been fortunate to speak with people such as Leslie Flint and a number of other physical mediums, and with their help I began to form an understanding of what it takes for Spirit to be able to manifest direct voice and physical phenomena. Clearly the medium does play an important part in such séances; the substance known as ectoplasm comes from the physical body of the medium. "Right," I hear you say, "then how come people have not seen or felt this ectoplasm?" But they have; in fact, scientists have also examined it.

Let us examine this substance from its very name "ectoplasm." (This word comes from the two Greek words ektos and plasma, which together mean exteriorized substance.) The word was coined by Dr. Charles Richet, a French professor of physiology. He had been investigating Spiritualism for a number of years and had witnessed ectoplasm emanating from mediums during séances. Over the centuries there have been many accounts of materializations, or the dead appearing to the living in a way that appeared miraculous. We can see this quite often in the Bible itself. On numerous occasions we have detailed reports of people from all walks of life testifying that they have witnessed, and have, in fact, actually touched loved ones who have died yet somehow managed to show themselves again in a physical form. How can this be? Ectoplasm! This substance has been extensively examined by many scientists, in particular by Baron von Schrenck Notzing, a German physician who spent many years researching mediums and conducting séances. He was given permission at some séances to remove or amputate small portions of ectoplasm for microscopic and chemical analysis. This, of course, puts the medium concerned at great risk, and one can only assume that the medium—and more important, Spirit—completely trusted the baron. For those technically minded here is part of what the baron concluded about ectoplasm. Chemical analysis: "colorless, slightly cloudy, fluid (thready), no smell; traces of cell detritus and sputum. Deposit, whitish. Reaction, slightly alkaline." Under "Microscopic Examination" he stated, "Numerous skin discs; some sputum-like bodies; numerous granulates of the mucous membrane; numerous minute particles of flesh; traces of 'sulphozyansaurem' potash. Apparently the dried residue weighed 8.60 grams Per liter, 3 grams Ash."

All this research is interesting if you're a scientist, perhaps, but to the majority of us what does it mean? It does go some way to bear out what most people are beginning to believe, that we humans are more than physical. It has long been suggested that apart from the physical body we have a secondary body, often referred to as the beta body. Many people maintain that this beta body is the seat of the soul, the *real* you! The beta body is connected to the physical body by what has frequently been referred to as "the silver cord" (which gets its name, by the way, from the biblical phrase "or ever the silver cord be loosed").

While the physical body is alive, the two are connected, and in some people this cord can be extremely elastic, allowing the beta body to occasionally roam far away from the physical body, while still being attached by the cord. Many people believe that this theory helps explain the many near-death experiences people have had. In some spiritually developed beings, as in the case of the late Italian monk Father Pio, the beta body is witnessed in one location when it was known that the monk was physically in another place. This phenomenon has also been said to be observed in the Indian mystic Sai Baba.

It is only when that silver cord is actually severed that death, as we understand it, occurs and the physical body ceases to be. But though our physical bodies may die, the beta, the real you, continues. It is the real you that some people known as mediums are able to connect with.

Physical mediums such as Leslie Flint have the blessing of having a developed, "loose" beta body, and it is from this beta body that the spirit world is able to draw the energy called ectoplasm and mold it into what has been called a temporary voice box. It is believed that this ectoplasmic voice box is what is used by spirits when they communicate in such a way as direct voice mediumship.

Clearly, ectoplasm and direct voice mediumship have to be investigated and documented further. But there are already hundreds of books at all levels dealing with physical mediumship, from scientific works to mediums' autobiographies. Many were written a number of years ago and some so long ago that we may rightly or wrongly question some of the claims made in these books in the light of modern "advanced" thinking. All I can say is that the scientific investigators of the twentieth century seemed a lot more diligent and thorough than some who have in recent years sought to pour scorn on all such investigations. After all, most of the miracles in the Bible can be explained and accepted once we understand what Spirit has been telling us since time began, that we do not die, not the *real* us! I find it rather strange how some people are happy to rely on faith, and that is their prerogative, believing in books written long ago and much altered by man. Yet when these same people are confronted with actual demonstrations of mediumistic ability they are often the first to scream objections and cite all sorts of misconstrued religious teachings about why such things should not be allowed to take place, when, really, such demonstrations would only prove what they already believed!

Fortunately, probably more than ever before in the Earth's history, we have a preponderance of people who can prove, day in and day out, that there is indeed life after so-called death. There are a number of "mental mediums," clairvoyants, clairaudients, and clairsentients, living all over the world. They range in ability from indifferent to outstanding. Of course, their reasons for performing séances and readings can also be sometimes questioned. Some may seek fame and money, but most genuinely wish to share what they have found to be true with others who seek their help.

CHAPTER 5

In My Father's House

The true meaning of religion is thus not simply morality, but morality touched by emotion.

—MATTHEW ARNOLD

While we do have more mediums alive in the world today than ever before, the standard of mediumship has, in general, dropped. The interest in this phenomenon has led many people to decide that they would like to become mediums, and though some of these people may have talent, they are frequently being brought to the public's attention before they are ready. Consequently, mental mediumship has had a rough time in the press, and often outstanding mediums are criticized and even abused by the media because of the antics of a few substandard people.

If only people realized that genuine mediums are among the most skeptical people in the universe. They often work hard—harder than anyone in the media ever would—to understand what is occurring around them. They check, question, and do not just accept what is told them. As proof, I'll offer my thoughts on how two outstanding well-known mediums approached having a sitting with me. They are James Van Praagh and John Edward.

In the fall of 1994 I was asked to give a lecture at the Learning Light Foundation in Orange County, California. I was asked if I would give a sitting to someone who had heard that I was visiting. I was told only the following: First, the sitting was important to the person. Second, the sitter would arrive at noon for a half-hour session. Third, the person's name was Jimmy. That's all I knew.

It actually would not have made much difference to me if the sitter had given his full name. I had never seen James Van Praagh before and, living mainly in England, I had not even heard of his name (all of this occurred before the hit television program *The Other Side* and even before the publication of his best seller *Talking to Heaven*), so what media attention James had already received I was unaware of. I will never reveal the contents of any sittings, and these two are no exception, but there are two things that have subsequently been mentioned by both James and myself, so I feel comfortable relating them here. One is the fact that Spirit told me the book he was then in the middle of writing would be important—and *Talking to Heaven* has certainly changed many people's lives! The other extraordinary incident was that James invited me to lunch right after his sitting. When I explained that I could not go as I had another appointment, James replied, "Oh, they will not come." I said he was crazy, as the next appointment had been booked months before and had already been paid for! But sure enough, the next appointment failed to show up. We went to lunch and found that although we had had very different lives we had many an experience in common. James had even met Leslie Flint. So it came about that James invited me to Hollywood to demonstrate with him at three of his hugely popular public demonstrations. James is a wonderful medium. He has the great gift of communicating personalities and feelings as well as giving evidence.

If James was cautious about revealing too much about himself before the reading, John Edward was downright secretive. In early 1998, my then organizer, Ursula Reeg, told me that a sitting had been booked that would have to be conducted on the telephone, as the sitter was far away and could not attend in person. Again I was given the time of the appointment and told that a John Esposito would call. I know that John has graciously and publicly recalled this reading at several of his sold-out public demonstrations, especially when I have been present, so I feel free to share this experience now. The telephone sitting of course meant that I could not see the person, and could therefore not be accused of waiting for his facial expression to change or of reading his body language. Now, the millions who have now seen John Edward on television will all agree that when he starts talking he can go like a machine gun! But the John I had on the telephone replied with unemotional Yeses or Nos. At some point in the reading John called his wife, Sandra, and asked her to listen in, as it was an emotional experience for all concerned. When the reading ended and John revealed his true name and who he really was, I immediately felt terrible, as I had never seen him work—I had barely heard of him at all! This of course was before his phenomenally successful television show and just before his first book was published. John kindly invited me to New York and introduced me to many new friends on the East Coast. He also invited me to join him on his many-city tour of the United States, organized by the Learning Annex. John explained that he was eager for people to see that others had similar gifts and that no one person, country, or religion had an exclusive hold on Spirit communication. John is enjoying much personal success at present. I cannot help but think that this is in part due to the way that he generously and genuinely followed the spiritual advice to "cast your bread upon the water and it will return tenfold." Which is another clue to what Spirit is trying to show us: Do things for the right reason and with a good heart and you will succeed.

So besides being skeptical and secretive, just what is it that we mediums do? Most, when asked, will take a stab at explaining the process. I have to say that I have sat through some hilarious explanations, some that were so complicated that I had to wonder whether, if they were indeed coming from Spirit, they did not want us to understand the process. In general, the more complex and complicated the explanation the further from the simple truth we seem to get. The key word for all mediums is vibration. Essentially, a medium is one who can change the vibration of his or her beta body. Some can do this without conscious thought and often "pick up" information without thinking about it in a way that's somewhat similar to intuition. Others can train themselves to adjust their frequency and tune in to the spirit world, like a radio looking for a signal. When it's attached to the physical body, the beta body vibrates more slowly. It's as if the beta body is being weighed down by a heavy overcoat. But when the silver cord is stretched and the beta body is separated from the physical, it vibrates much faster. And when we die, our beta body is completely disconnected from the physical, and its vibration increases even more. The majority of us cannot see or detect these different levels of vibrations—in particular, the extremely high vibrations after the physical body dies. This is not surprising, since most of our lives we are fed the untruth that "when you are dead you are dead." Most of us are all but brainwashed from early childhood, by misguided parents, religious leaders, and peer pressure, to only accept what we can see and hear. Every dog knows that the world is full of interesting sounds outside the human hearing range, so why do we humans limit ourselves by only trusting our physical experiences? Are we not alive, the same as the dog? I firmly believe that we humans can still learn a lot of spiritual truths from the animal kingdom.

What if we could change our way of thinking, so that we do not fear death but acknowledge it as just as wonderful as the birth into this life, acknowledge that the "real" us does continue, that no matter what stage of spiritual evolution we may be at we can always progress? This is another important point that spirit communication tries to tell us. If this is so, then how we lead our lives, how we react and deal with one another, should be our paramount consideration in this life in order that we may continue to spiritually progress.

As Ivy Northage was so adamant about pointing out, the medium's primary purpose is to attempt to prove that life continues after so-called death. With mental mediumship the communicating spirit actively cooperates in the process. Just as the medium must raise the vibrations of his or her beta body to communicate with spirits, the communicating spirit, the instigator, must slow his or her vibration (beta body) so that the medium can make contact. Depending on what gift the medium has best developed, the medium then obtains information that is relayed to the sitter.

The sitter's part is to confirm or deny the information that comes through, where possible with a simple Yes or No answer. The sitter also provides the emotional link to people they have known who are now in the spirit world. Love is essential for a medium to operate successfully—Spirit senses the emotions and can be powerfully drawn to them.

Mediumship in all its forms can be objective and subjective. There has been much discussion whether sitters and mediums alike actually see those who have died in the physical sense or whether it is just a vision or image that they perceive in their minds. Both have been documented as having occurred. The accounts of "ghost sightings" all around the world are too numerous to discard—especially since the descriptions have a consistent theme running through them. They are often described as "luminous figures" that "appear almost see-through" and that often "disappear quickly" (sustaining the lower vibration would be just as difficult and exhausting for the ghost as raising the vibration would be for the medium). What people have been witnessing when they see ghosts are spontaneous sightings of the beta (spirit) body, which is in fact a whole double of our physical body.

Now, some mediums working objectively are able to accurately describe the details of deceased loved ones with amazing accuracy. You will often hear many mediums say in a public demonstration, "I see your mother or father standing near you," and then go on to give often very detailed descriptions. I remember at one demonstration that a young woman came through from Spirit and showed me clearly a tattoo that would not, let us say, have been visible to anyone unless that person had been *very* well acquainted with her. Now, I had never met this person, but it was great proof to her husband sitting in the audience! This type of mediumship is called objective clairvoyance. A medium working subjectively, on the other hand, will often say things like, "This feels like Mother." Often, such mediums are getting impressions in picture form and are literally having an image impressed on their minds and are more aware of emotions and feelings than actually physical descriptions. There can be much evidence gained from both ways of working. For example, how many people did not actually know their grandparents but know about them from their parents? It would be rather pointless to go through detailed descriptions if the recipients had never actually seen the person communicating, but it would make sense to communicate details about the people, their character, their personalities, and what they had been like, to those who had only heard about these ancestors. These, too, should be checkable facts.

Mediums working clairaudiently (where the medium actually hears what Spirit is saying) are very interesting. As with clairvoyance, clairaudience can be both objective and subjective. The most famous recent clairaudient was Doris Stokes, who for many years worked both as a clairvoyant and a clairaudient. Though she was more than capable at both, her fame spread due to the accuracy of her clairaudient gift. Doris claimed to actually hear the voices of spirits. She wrote numerous books about this phenomena and thrilled audiences around the world. I watched her demonstrate several times, and although all of us mediums can get it wrong sometimes (we are, after all only human!), more often than not when Doris said something like, "I have your daughter here, and she tells me her name is Ruth," the recipient would not only confirm the fact that they had a daughter in Spirit but also that that indeed was her name. I am in no doubt that Doris Stokes worked as an objective clairaudient. Those working as subjective clairaudients, on the other hand, are often heard to say, "It sounds like," followed by an approximation of the sound that is being impressed on them—in the case above, a clairaudient might say, "Your daughter's name is something like Booth? Tooth?" What subjective clairaudients hear is usually very close to what is trying to be transmitted. Clairaudients can come up with the most startling evidence, the accuracy being such that some people often look for other means of explanation. A few years ago, I was at a demonstration given by John Edward to a large group of media execs and personalities. John suddenly announced that he was hearing something about the "Gutenberg Bible." After a short while a well-known actress in the audience stood up and announced that while flying she often listened to an audiotape of the Gutenberg Bible to alleviate her nervousness. In fact, she had arrived at the event directly from the airport and had the tape in her bag.

Now had John said, "I hear the name 'Bill or Mary'," I might have thought, "Well, that's a name that could apply to many people," but he clearly heard Gutenberg Bible. What is the likelihood of that?

The clairsentient works mainly with feeling and again can be aware of feelings being impressed and can actually feel certain sensations. This is particularly useful when trying to convey cause of dying or what temperament the communicating person had. As a medium who tends to work objectively, I often feel a small jolt in the heart when spirit communicators want it known that they passed because of a heart attack or ailment, or I'll develop a brief headache if the cause of death was head trauma. Subjective mediums will instead be more generally directed to the heart region or feel the need to touch and talk about the head area.

The very best-developed mediums, although they may well be especially proficient in one of the above ways of communicating, usually use a combination of the three gifts. Most of the mediums we are witnessing now in the media fall into this category. Some of us have also at times smelled certain fragrances that have also been readily identified with a deceased loved one. (I feel this kind of information should be used to confirm a communicating spirit only after all the other facts have been established.) Cigarette smoke is the easiest but I have witnessed mediums being able to identify individually named scents or perfumes that passed relatives had preferred. In itself this does not prove continuation of life, but added to a personal description and other validated facts, such as names, this gift can help to establish that a loved one is really trying to communicate, has conscious memory, and can create smells that we may readily associate with the loved one.

Because we live in a time where there are so many mediums on television and the radio, I'm often asked if anyone can become a medium. I believe that while everyone can benefit from the discipline and knowledge that can be gained from attending workshops and classes, not everyone can or will become an effective medium. Most of us, for example, can learn to carry a tune, tinkle the ivories, or communicate through the written word, but Pavarotti, Beethoven, or Shakespeare this does not make. Surely, whatever we choose to do in this life, we should aim to do it to the best of our ability. And I believe that any attempt to understand the process of communication with Spirit can lead to good, so I feel it should actively be encouraged. It would certainly lead to more harmony in our world. No matter what boundaries of race, culture, or belief we place on ourselves, we all have souls and we are all one.

Unfortunately, some mediums, like many religious and cult leaders, begin to think that the way that they have found to work is the only way and do not leave room for people's unique gifts and methods. This is very sad and leads to a lot of confusion among those who are truly in search of the teachings of Spirit. It also provides a field day for cynics, who happily point out that mediums, Spiritualists, and all other religions tend to shoot themselves in the foot. In one breath we bring forth messages of hope from Spirit, and in the next we sometimes get dogmatic, saying that this way or that is the correct way. The truth is that, as a very great soul and the foremost exponent of mediumship in its highest form has already pointed out, "In my father's house, there are many mansions."

As an ordained minister I am well aware of the contentious—to some *offensive*—statement that Jesus was a medium. Yet only when we understand the workings of the natural laws will we know that this is the clearest explanation that we have of the phenomena of his healing and teaching ministry. This does not in any way suggest that any medium before or since was or is of the same spiritual development as Jesus. Remember, he came to show us the way. Most credible mediums I know would wince at the thought that their work may be held in comparison to that of Jesus. And if you meet a medium who makes the claim that his or her work should be judged of the same quality, run like mad!

When we look at the Bible through spiritual eyes with knowledge of the natural laws, many of the Bible's mysteries and miracles can be explained. We can see how the walls of Jericho fell due to vibration. When Jesus brought Lazarus back from the dead, it is clear that as a highly developed medium, he could see that "the silver cord" had not been finally broken. By using his gift of clairvoyance he could see that the beta body was still attached to the physical, therefore he was able to restore Lazarus' health using his supreme healing gift. If that silver cord had been broken the healing could not have taken place. Not even a master could restore life. The gift of life belongs to the Supreme Being some call God, others Allah, some Yahweh. There are many names but all describe the same being. Only the creator has the ability to manifest life.

Throughout the Old and New Testaments there is talk of voices, healings, visions, seers, prophets, messengers, and appearances of people known to be dead. (Just read the account of the apostles in the upper room and doubting Thomas, then read a credible account of a physical phenomena séance, and I ask you to explain the difference!) Read Revelations and you will think Nostradamus was not so odd. Read the account of Moses and the Ten Commandments. The dream of Elijah. Throughout the Bible you will see examples of clairvoyance, clairaudience, and clairsentience. It's all there if only we read it correctly—and with an open mind.

We can even see that progress is open to all. Take St. Paul, for example. Here was a man who was, in his early days, what we would call a mercenary. Yet he went on to "see the light" and became a great teacher. I ask those who believe that mediumship is wicked to read again the letter from St. Paul to the Corinthians. Nowhere is it more clearly written that the gift of mediumship should be recognized and cherished. I fail to see how anyone reading and believing in this great book can deny the existence of life after death.

Sadly there are those who, for whatever reason, seek to divide instead of unite. No doubt there are some who truly believe that their way alone can help mankind. Recently in Long Island, New York, I went to demonstrate spirit communication at a high school. The event was a fundraiser for the school, yet the board of directors had been forced to issue a statement distancing themselves from the evening's events. A local Baptist minister had been complaining weeks before my arrival about "these evil mediums and wicked spirits." He even went so far as to have leaflets printed, one of which he handed me, not knowing that I was the evil medium. I am not so sure that I would entrust my spiritual education to someone who could not see "evil" when it was standing in front of him.

Of course, not all religions and religious leaders are so close-minded. I had an excellent opportunity in one sitting to question Spirit about what happens to the various religions and faiths that we adhere to here on Earth when we make that transition called death. A man had come to see me, and during the sitting, his father communicated with us. From the outset I was aware and a little concerned that his father in Spirit made it obvious that he had been a minister. I clearly saw his clothing. At the end of the sitting I asked my client whether he minded if I asked his father a question. He said, "Go right ahead." My question was,

"What happens to the different religions when we pass, are we all separated, Christians in one place, Jews, Muslims, Hindus, Buddhists, and so forth in other places?"

His answer to me was that I should look toward the corner of the room we were sitting in. I can only describe that I saw the outline of many human forms walking toward a light. And it appeared that on reaching this light they took off what I presumed to be their overcoats. "Is it warm over there? Is that why they are removing their coats?" I said, trying to make some common sense of this vision. The minister from Spirit replied, "No. What is being shed are all the embellishments man has added to the one truth." He went on to state that many of the religions we accept on this Earth pertain to the physical (the food laws of the Jewish religion, the contraceptive rules of the Catholic Church, and so forth). On the occasion of death we leave all these things behind and take with us only that which is the kernel of truth at the heart of most religions, the importance of the way we have treated one another. He went on to state that the world's religions were but maps for this life—maps that many people need and rely on. Our friend from Spirit then went on to explain how Spirit viewed the Earth plane with regard to religion. He told me that they saw the Earth as a great school for education and that among people of all religions (and those without any), there were those who excelled. These were the people who questioned, kept an open mind, and sought to advance the development of their souls. But in all religions there were those who stamped their feet and said, "My way or no way." These souls, he explained, were those in the kindergarten.

My client was most impressed that his father, who had been very much of the "hellfire and brimstone" fundamentalist Baptist faith, had progressed from his narrow view. It was not lost on me that it was a Baptist church member who had turned me away from formally organized religion (and juice and cookies!) as a boy, and here was a former minister explaining the essence of religions to me.

CHAPTER 6

So What Have the Spirits Told Me?

If you have knowledge, let others light their candles at it.
—MARGARET FULLER

My work as a medium has been an incredible journey to date, and I am in no doubt that although I may have traveled far there is much more to learn. The classes I attended were without question pivotal to my understanding of how mediumship works. But it has been the thousands of sittings both private and public that have been the true source of my knowledge of how we are ultimately responsible for all our actions and consequently therefore the reactions.

I would never be a person to "just accept the word of another," whether that person be alive in the physical sense or communicating from the spirit realms. I have always tried to be consistent in my investigations, and I have to say it has been shown to me that whenever my questions were in earnest, Spirits have done their utmost to cooperate and answer in definite ways.

Often the questions I had came from my own natural curiosity. What happens at the point of death? Are suicides really punished? Why do some die so young? What becomes of evil people? To these questions and many more I sought the answers, but I also experienced periods when it seemed that people in similar situations did their best to seek a sitting with me. For a while I assumed that some of these people were connected and perhaps some did pass my name on to friends and relatives, but traveling the world as I do, speaking with people of different cultures and often with people who have no language in common, it has dawned on me that not only has there been some form of concerted effort on the part of Spirit to answer my questions, by bringing people to me, but through its consistency it has attempted to tell the truth to many and diverse people.

There have been times when it seemed that people who had similar experiences found their way to me. At one point in my development as a medium people from America, India, England, and elsewhere all seemed to have known someone who had "taken themselves over," or committed suicide as it is ignorantly called. It took a while for me to realize that at this period not only was I being bombarded with Spirits who had passed in such a way, but people from different countries with no connections to one another were somehow being guided to me. What I began to notice was that although each sitting was unique, with individual and personal details, the majority had common threads. Although I have vowed never to reveal the contents of any particular sitting, I feel it is right and may be of interest and help to others to share some of these common threads. Perhaps it will help others to understand what Spirit has been trying to show over the centuries. If it assists anyone who has narrow views on such topics to consider a different viewpoint, then I feel that in passing on these findings, not only have I acknowledged the lessons but also I confirm that the trust Spirit placed in me was well-founded.

It should not be a surprise to anyone who read the first chapters of this book to find that one of the first questions to be answered by Spirit was, "What happens to suicides?" I have to say this was not one of my conscious questions, but after the event with my uncle I suppose the thought was buried somewhere in my mind. We are all aware of what the various religions have had to say about those who take themselves over. It has been my experience that the attitude ranges from pity to an assertion of their downright evilness. I never could envisage a God of unconditional love who would slap and cast aside a child for getting something wrong. It just seems unreal that anyone should be condemned to hell at the very point where that person most needs love and understanding. After hundreds of sittings involving suicides I have come to the conclusion that most religious institutions here in the physical world have it wrong. I can easily understand—and agree with—their position on the sanctity and preciousness of life. But their take on suicides is an example of ruling through fear, which is just one of the mistakes many religions are now paying for.

SUICIDE

It seems obvious to me that the people who know most about suicide are those who have experienced it, and those who have been affected by their actions.

Do they regret their actions? Every sitting I have conducted, the communicating Spirit has replied Yes to that question, not so much because of how they had harmed themselves but for the pain that they inflicted on those they now realize truly loved them. They feel regret for the relatives and friends and loved ones whom they witness being in pain and distress on the Earth plane. I am told by Spirit that all are met at the point of physical death, and suicides are no exception. Normally, when someone passes over a great crowd comes together to celebrate their homecoming—it can be a wonderful celebration. In the case of suicide, however, one or two loving souls, often close relatives who love them unconditionally and who have already passed, meet them and explain that yes they have indeed reached home, but they are asked to look back and see what they have left behind. What is it that they see? Invariably they witness their loved ones in anguish, often they see parents or relatives berating themselves, asking what else they could have done. "If only we had listened," is a thought they often hear. This pain is often followed by anger—Spirits witness our anger, they see it as red sparks flying from us.

This type of bereavement is cruel in that it is hard for those on the physical side of life to understand why anyone, especially someone they knew so well, should want to end their life. After all, the majority of people, no matter what their beliefs, are not 100 percent sure whether there is anything after death. Those who have trusted and believed the various religions are now told that the act of suicide is an abomination and that those who committed such acts go to hell. No wonder there has been such torment over the centuries over such transitions.

When people have come to see me seeking to find out what has happened to their loved ones, obviously I have no idea before their visit what information they are seeking. But it does seem that in the case of suicides, the Spirits are most anxious to communicate. What usually is the difficulty is the loved ones here on the physical plane. It is they who have to overcome shock, anger, pain, the sense of uselessness, and often, unfounded guilt. Once it has been explained by those who meet our loved ones on the other side that their acts were like arrows to the very heart of those who truly love them, they are eager to communicate, to try to let their relatives and loved ones know that they are all right. But grief and sorrow, guilt and anger are like a glass wall to spirit communication—such emotions are almost impenetrable. At the same time, though, these emotions are often necessary stages of bereavement, a process that is good for us, and one we all have to work through at some time. Often I have found that the person sitting with me has come to that part in grief where "they just need to know that so and so is okay." This usually we find out. After the Spirit has given much detail and proven the existence of life after death and that they are in fact who they say they are, they will often describe how they watched the tears and distress they cause and the anger they see. It is often when we have exhausted all these emotions and processes that the glass wall disappears and the healing begins.

I've also found that the healing occurs on both sides. Can you imagine proving to a grieving mother that her son was not condemned to fire and hell, that he does continue to live, and that there was no judgment except for his own true regret for the pain he caused and the opportunities his actions caused him to miss out on in this life? That mother can continue her life, not easily, but continue she will, without guilt or shame, in the knowledge that her son is fine and continues his evolvement in the spirit world.

It is a fact that we are all on the Earth plane for our own education and evolvement, which can come through learning from or teaching others. Every aspect of our life has a meaning, nothing is by chance, and yet we have free will in all our decisions. We do not escape anything by the mere act of dying. If we have the lesson of responsibility here and decide we do not want to learn it, we may feel that by "taking ourselves over" we might escape such a chore. But we do not!

One of the other common threads is that most Spirits that have taken themselves over go on to tell us what they are doing in the spirit world. How often I have heard a message, "Tell them I am working with children, and have a lot of patience now," only to be informed by the sitter, "Well about time, he/she never had any here!" Or, "Tell them I am so busy, there is so much to do, every moment is a surprise, I am happy." The sitter's reply is often, "The reason he killed himself was that he thought there was nothing more for him to do, that no one needed him, and he was miserable." If only these people could have seen that such lessons were available here on the Earth plane, so much pain could have been averted.

All of us are individual, and yet we are connected. The more we agree to take on our individual lessons and responsibilities and learn from them, the better it has to be for mankind as a whole. Spirit has shown me that it is for no man to judge another for his failings. We cannot condemn someone for getting things wrong, for being afraid, or for feeling that life has no purpose. At the same time, though, we cannot condone the act of suicide, because if everyone learned their lessons on the Earth plane, no matter how great or how harsh those lessons might be, I believe mankind could take a big step forward spiritually.

I will not condemn the person who decides on suicide, but I would ask anyone thinking of such an option to please consider the consequences of their actions as they affect others. If you really cannot think of one person who will be affected by your action, would you consider the fact that no matter how great a lesson you face, someone, somewhere is waiting to learn how you will deal with a situation; don't deny yourself or your fellow man the benefit of your expertise in dealing with your individual task.

Many people are able to say, "I understand what you are going through," to someone in a lot of pain, or who is going through a tough time. Perhaps they do. Maybe they had similar experiences, but can anyone truthfully say to another, "I *know* what you are going through"? How do we know—how *can* we know—what another person is experiencing? We all deal with this life's problems in different ways, and what to one person may seem an insurmountable problem appears to another as a challenge; a disaster to some is a mere hiccup to others. But really, is there any situation so insoluble that it is worth missing out on this great adventure we call life? Beyond what appears dark there is always light.

I will use a quotation from my guide Ramadahn to illustrate Spirit's view of the challenges that come man's way: "An oyster takes an irritation and makes of it a pearl. How many pearls can you make in a life-time?"

THE PASSING OF A CHILD: A PARENT'S NIGHTMARE

I must confess, throughout my work and still today, I have found dealing with parents whose children have died to be positively traumatic. Though I have no personal experience of this kind of loss, I have always had questions about it. Why should this happen? What is the point in such a brief life? How cruel can any God be to allow a child to pass when there was so much to do, such hope, where there was so much promise shown? What kind of creator watches parents as they invest unconditional love in their children, only to deal them the catastrophic blow of snatching these young people before any of us were ready?

The whole point of living, as far as many of us are concerned, is to live a long, healthy, and useful life. Where is the sense in someone passing at a young age before they have gained any experiences? What parent can ever contemplate having a child die before he or she does? It is every parent's nightmare. It is also an experience that competent and experienced mediums can discern very quickly. In my case, because I tend to look at the beta body rather than the physical one, I sometimes see scars around the heart area of the person who has come to me for a reason. No matter how long ago the event, the scars are always there when I am seeing a parent whose child has passed. It makes no difference if it is one person seeing me or if I am demonstrating to a hall of a thousand people: The scars will show. This used to worry me. I often considered, Is this an ongoing experience? Does anyone really recover from such tragedy? Some never do, but many can at least find peace, knowledge, and understanding from the teachings that Spirit brings via the instrument known as a medium. I consider this part of my work to be one of the most important, enriching, and spiritually rewarding, and I am in awe each time I see someone wearing these scars, or as I now call them, badges of unconditional love.

Linking parents with their children in Spirit is, as I have said, traumatic for me, but it also has given me much understanding of why we are here and what this life is really all about. In nearly all such cases I have found that both the children involved and the parents are exceptional souls, and their lessons are very much of the teacher/pupil nature, but not one that most people would assume.

Very early on in my development, I first started to question why so many people die at a young age. As I found that many people were seeking me who had this experience I began to question Spirit not only for my own curiosity, but because I wanted some answers that

I could pass to these often inconsolable parents. I have met many amazing and brave mothers and fathers over the years, but in Los Angeles I met a special lady called Nancy.

Nancy was to become somewhat of a champion for my work. She initially sought me out because her son had passed, and she told me later that the comfort and peace she received from the sittings she had with me was something she wanted others to experience. There were, however, some obstacles. One was that Nancy was a member of Compassionate Friends, a bereavement group that has many chapters throughout the world. One of the organizers of Nancy's group was against mediums, fearing that they just held out false hope. Another was that her husband Charles could not accept that such communication was possible, but being a devoted and loving husband he agreed to sit through sittings and demonstrations. No matter what information came through, and I will state that it was some of the best evidence I have ever received from Spirit, Charles was not going to be totally convinced. Other members of Nancy's family were strong in their Jewish beliefs and they would have nothing whatsoever to do with mediums. Despite these obstacles, Nancy and Charles were kindness itself to me and to the many parents Nancy was to introduce to me.

So here we have a lady whose religion did not encourage consulting mediums, whose husband did not fully accept what it was that she was seeking, and whose main source of comfort, her support group, did not approve of her speaking to other members about the comfort she had found through Spirit contact. But despite all these obstacles, Nancy was a mother, and when she was told that her compassionate friends group would not be willing to officially invite me or any medium, Nancy set about organizing group demonstrations in her home. It was from these small gatherings that my name was handed to groups first around the Los Angeles area and then farther afield. I always felt a special bond with Nancy, for despite all of the pain and emotion she had gone through, she always had a smile, something funny to say, and she went out of her way to help any parent who sought help or guidance. I learned much about strength and courage from her, and this enables me to understand to some degree the pain that parents suffer when a child dies. As a result, I was shocked when Charles got a message to me to say that Nancy had passed. I always believed we were of the same soul group and had the same mission, yet I often wondered—after she had passed—why I had no prior knowledge of her illness. How could I not have known, and why did she not tell me herself? Together I know we helped many. Spirit tells us that there are no coincidences and that a death in this life is a birth in the next. Nancy is a great lady and a great mother and passed on October 18th, my birthday. I believe that this was a confirmation of our accord.

So What Have the Spirits Told Me?

One of the first things that Spirit gave me when I began asking, "Why do children die?" was a poem. I at first thought it trite. It is only four lines and just twenty-six words long. However over the years, after many sittings and much understanding I see the beauty and truth that is captured by its simplicity.

> *This lovely bud, so young and pure,*
> *No grief, or sorrow knew,*
> *Came but to show the parents how to love,*
> *And then to heaven withdrew.*

It is my understanding that the souls of children who pass before their parents are highly developed spiritually. It is often the case that the younger someone passes the more spiritually progressed that person is. It is these children who come to bring out the love in their parents, for once experienced, that kind of love can never be ignored. These children are our teachers. Our souls need to experience many lessons, and what greater lesson is there than love? The love that is so often between parents and their children is unique, and the reason many are totally bereft after such a passing is that we cannot believe what we have been shown we are capable of.

This is the reason we grieve so much. It took a child to show us that it is all right to show our true feelings, but first we have to have the experience of what those feelings are. Often we take things for granted, and it is only when they are not within our physical grasp that we recognize what we have. If this has happened to you, you have indeed been "touched by an angel."

It will come as no surprise to anyone who has known a child who has passed that everyone agrees that the child in question was exceptional. Parents adore them, teachers describe them as bright, grandparents worship them, often they are magnets for other people, and they sometimes seem to be "older than their years." Their lives tend to be like a stone hitting a pond: They make a big splash in this world and no matter how short or long their physical life, theirs is like a ripple that touches many. As a medium I acknowledge them as "old souls in young bodies."

We have to understand that no matter how we feel or tend to describe our relationships (people will often refer, for example, to "my son," or "our daughter"), we can never own another person, and children are no exception. Although this soul was entrusted to you, he or she does not become yours to possess exclusively, even though the love that you show each other forms the very bond that will link you forever. Your children in spirit are eternally grateful for the experience of love that you have shown, and we should in turn be thankful for the many lessons they come to teach us.

Often I have heard during a sitting from a child who had passed with some dreadful or lingering disease; I guarantee that at some point during such sittings, after all the evidence and facts have been delivered, one or both of the parents will speak of the bravery of their child, of how brave their child was to fight his or her ailments. This is not just seeing things through rose-tinted glasses. Children by nature do not fear. It is we adults who instill fear in them. That children can show us the lesson of courage when so ill, that they show trust in those that love and care for them, and that often, despite the odds of recovery given by medical science, they persevere in their fight to live this life surely should make us want to live every experience in what we call this life. Are such souls not our teachers?

I am not a fatalist. I do not believe that it is written in the spirit world that at ten years of age this will happen or at fifteen years that will occur and that all of our lives are preordained. I do, however, believe that we all have a certain amount of energy to complete our purpose here and that when that purpose is achieved it is our time to return to the spirit realms. When someone touches our life briefly but profoundly, how much greater are the lessons? It is then our responsibility to honor such souls, to heed their teachings and apply them to our lives. In this way we can see that progressed souls do incarnate as children to teach us.

I am afraid that I have lost count of the many sittings I have conducted where "accidents" were the cause of a child's passing. I do not believe in accidents. Yes, it is true, if one of our loved ones has to die, then of course we want to be with that person, with our children especially, but naturally we would move heaven and Earth itself if we were present and could prevent such things occurring. Often this type of passing is instantaneous, and the fact that the child does not physically suffer is of some comfort. We must remember, though, that every action has its lesson for someone. In the many cases of children passing through, say, the direct or indirect actions of another, Spirit considers this a true crime, for we are all responsible for our own conduct. Society can do what it feels is right to punish such criminals, but the real price is paid when the perpetrators themselves pass: Then they have to stand before their victims and explain why they denied them the experience of this life. I am told it is the most humbling of experiences, but inevitably the progressed soul forgives. It is another lesson the progressed souls teach us—forgiveness.

The Nazarene was only thirty-three years old when he passed. An undoubtedly progressed soul, he came to show mankind the way, to teach, and he did so with free will. But he was also someone's son. God does not allow these tragedies to "happen" randomly. Let us understand that if you have been touched by such tragedy, it was because a very progressed soul knew that you are special enough to warrant them spending their energy with you. That somehow, you needed to know the lesson of love and that their need to experience love could come from you, a parent who could give that love to a child, your teacher.

DISEASE

I have had the opportunity to give sittings to many people over the years, and in them people inevitably raise the question of diseases. Why do we get illnesses and disease? Why is it that some people suffer more than others? Is it just chance that some people are more prone to certain diseases than others?

We are all aware that certain actions on our part increase the risk of our contracting various illnesses and disease, and there are of course decisions we can make to reduce those chances. But I am now firmly of the belief that many of our ailments are self-induced. I am not stating that I think people go around consciously wanting to be ill, but my experiences with Spirit have shown me that some people are susceptible to certain health conditions but ignore the warning signs. If we only take action and recognize what our soul is trying to tell us via our physical body, we can lead full and healthy lives.

The soul has a purpose, and it knows the purpose for which it came to inhabit the physical body. But when the soul sees that the physical or human part of us is not cooperating in that purpose, it becomes sick. Disease, meaning "ill at ease," is caused by a friction or stress between body and spirit—when the physical body doesn't conform to the lessons the beta body wishes to teach. Many illnesses can be avoided, and while our doctors and psychiatrists with their knowledge and

95

medicines can help balance our bodies, it is really up to us to keep ourselves balanced.

Our thoughts and actions are imprinted in every cell of our bodies, and if we get an accumulation of negative energy because of these thoughts and actions, that negative energy will eventually show up on our physical body. Take, for example, a man who thinks the only way to be a man is to never show his emotions: How often do we hear of such people having heart attacks? The heart is the seat of our emotional self, and it is good to express your emotions. Let the people whom you care about know you love them. Not only does it help you to deal with your emotions, but parents will also educate their children that it is healthy to be emotionally expressive. Many people are not fortunate enough to have a warning before going into cardiac arrest, but I have witnessed a complete change in attitude in many people who have heart attacks and survive them. So why wait for the warning? It is a balancing act between body and spirit, and mind is the coordinator. Think correct thoughts and correct actions follow.

I have spoken with many in the spirit world who have given their account of their illness—for example, cancer. We are aware of the different forms of cancer and its causes, but I am convinced that many cancers are, in fact, created by the mind. Again, no one would actively wish for this experience, but some of the negativity generated by our thoughts is very deep-seated. How many people go through life believing they have been wronged, perhaps through a divorce they never wanted or expected? Even though, out of necessity, people who feel cheated or upset one way or another seem, to all outward appearance, to get on with life, deep down they still harbor resentment. We may even go through days, months, or years without consciously thinking of this—which is truly frightening. What time bomb are we incubating by holding on to negative experiences? We have to live our lives, and not dwell on the past, but we should not live them in regret. Even from seemingly unfair situations we can learn. Often I have had messages come from Spirit telling people who have experienced divorce that, although it may have been an unpleasant situation to endure, they learned a lot about themselves. They may have learned that they were loyal, loving, good at making excuses, supportive . . . but maybe also a bit naïve. Now where is the badness in this? When undergoing an unpleasant experience, learn what you can from it, thank the person who brought you that lesson, and let that person go on his or her way. My guide Ramadahn told me long ago: "Don't look back, you will get a stiff neck mentally."

Not every negative thought ends in disease, of course, but we do create many of our situations. I well remember a very big lesson for me. In December 1995 I broke my leg. It was a particularly nasty break, being a double fracture of the fibula and tibia of the right leg. It came at what I believed to be the worst possible time. I was at one of my busiest periods, as I was being invited everywhere, people were crying out for development classes—and it seems stupid now, but there was almost a race on between various mediums to have books published and videos made. Although I was well known in some places I was getting more and more frustrated as it seemed that various publishing houses approached me only to pass me over for someone who had more media exposure. I found it all very stressful but believed Spirit had other plans for me, and in this way I thought I had dealt with my frustration. It was only after the accident and while speaking with my friends Lilia Logette and Barbara Simons, of the Center for Human Development in Florida, that Barbara asked me, "Did you break the right leg?" When I replied, "Yes," Barbara gave a very accurate analysis of what she believed had occurred. Barbara told me that there must be some area in my life that I felt frustration with or in which I had the feeling that I was "not going forward with something." She explained that in spiritual harmony terms the right leg is the one we go forward with in life and the left is the one we use when we follow through with things. Therefore the deep-seated frustration I felt at not moving forward with my work as a medium eventually showed itself in physical form. I can also report that when you have a broken leg, you have plenty of time to reflect and try to get things right.

There are a multitude of lessons to learn from disease, and not all of them are for the individual who suffers it. I now know that some souls incarnate, live their full purpose, and then in their manner of passing give their loved ones a great opportunity to learn. Never was this brought home to me more than in Los Angeles. I was giving a public demonstration and a young man from Spirit was communicating; his mother and sister were in the audience, and after various pieces of evidence were given, including his name, I felt really quite dreadful all over my body. I have witnessed the physical sensations of most passings but this was a feeling of being completely drained, an experience I had never had before. I asked in my mind, what was this sensation? Immediately I knew, it was AIDS. I asked the mother if she would mind if I stated what I believed was the cause of her son's passing. The mother told me she had no objections to others' knowing. What followed was quite a remarkable story. This young man was gay, and most of his life some members of the family had ostracized him because of his lifestyle. On finding that he was HIV positive and developing AIDS he had no one to turn to, as many of his friends had also passed or were busy with their lives. When his family found out, without hesitation and acting as one the whole family rallied around him and nursed him through his illness to his passing. It was a beautiful message when he said that he came to hold his mother's hand because when he had really needed it they were all there for him. If I remember correctly he said, "My family passed the test of rising above prejudice and fear, I am eternally grateful for their love and through my passing condition, showing them what they are capable of."

It is without doubt that our thoughts have power, and that when we dwell on the negative we attract that which is negative. We can literally think ourselves ill. If that's true, then clearly we can think ourselves well. It is without doubt easier to follow the spiral downward when bad things happen to us. How often do we say, "Why me? What have I done to deserve this?" The answer is that the real you—your soul—can learn from such an experience. When confronted with a disease, we tend to put on a brave face, go to pieces, or be defiant in the face of disease. Yet looking to the Bible again, we can find some wonderful advice: "Go within" . . . "Be silent and know" . . . "The kingdom of heaven is within." All the answers to our ills *are* within us. Ideally, we'd like to eliminate all negative thoughts and actions from our lives completely, but we are, when all is said and done, human, and we live in a world with other humans. It is this human part of us that needs to be aware that our thoughts are the seeds from which our actions germinate. Consequently we are also in part responsible for the reactions to our actions. Send out love and it will come back, and its power will overwhelm you. Send out hate and it too will return and probably knock you off your feet!

I am sure some people reading this will justifiably say, "I have never felt animosity toward anyone nor have I harbored any serious resentment, and yet I am ill myself." I ask you to reflect for a few moments on some of the sayings we all use, keeping in mind that our thoughts are imprinted in every cell of our body. Have you in the past set the following seeds in your subconscious mind?

"I don't want to hear it."

"Get off my back."

"I've bitten off more than I can chew."

"My back is to the wall."

"My heart is heavy with grief."

"He is breaking my heart."

"Shoulder responsibility."

"I feel it in my bones."

"I turned a blind eye to it."

All these and many more sayings are in everyday use, and if any are favorites of yours you are heading for problems—for every time you utter one of these statements, you are imprinting that feeling throughout your entire body. If you already have a problem with someone or are facing a tough challenge, be still and go within, acknowledge your failings, love and forgive yourself and anyone who may have caused you grief or harm. Send love and forgiveness to them or the suffering continues. Let us be conscious of our thoughts and how we can strive to keep them in accord with our soul's purpose. In this way I do believe many of the diseases of this world could be eradicated.

CHALLENGED?

How often have people with so-called physical handicaps been shunned or treated badly just because someone else who believes him- or herself to be "perfect" saw them as "different." The soul when it incarnates chooses the right body for its mission. Many wonderful souls have chosen a so-called disabled body because it suited their lesson or teachings. Think of Helen Keller, Beethoven, or Socrates—all had physical problems, yet each showed how it was the spirit—not the physical body—that triumphed over such challenges. The world would be a poorer place without all these wonderful souls.

This belief that anything less than "physical perfection" is unacceptable is clearly wrong. This was a lesson brought home to me while visiting a spiritual center that also has a special-needs school attached to it. A lady had made an appointment to see me, and she had brought along her two young children who she expected were going to wait while Mummy had her sitting. The lady had never seen me before, and as I passed her on my way to my room I heard her say the following: "Now I want you both to be good and wait for Mummy, because if you act up you could be punished and come back in another life like those poor children down the hall." To say I was stunned would be an understatement. The lady did not get her sitting. I am not sure she needed it, but we did spend some time together during which I pointed out that the only people likely to be in any way crippled were her children, emotionally and mentally, if they were taught such rubbish.

Whenever someone has a physical or mental challenge have you ever noticed that another part of the body or personality is compensated? This occurs because the soul is perfect, and even if one part of the physical body does not function, the soul remains radiant and shows its beauty in a pronounced way in another. Anyone who has had the experience of meeting someone with Down's syndrome will know that these are some of the most loving people in the world.

One of the most startling lessons Spirit gave me was that the blind can "see." I was in Munich, Germany. At the time my organizer was Frau Ronnie Marmorstein, a lady who has a lot of experience with mediums, since in the past she has hosted Gaye Muir and the brilliant psychic artist Coral Polge, among others. Ronnie was also my translator for my private sittings, since many of the people who were booked spoke little English. I was also due later that day to give a workshop, part of which was on the healing power of color. I had done this workshop many times and had been wracking my brains for new information most of the morning. At noon Ronnie announced we had one more sitting before lunch, and when the man arrived it was clear that he needed some help to sit down. After my usual two or three minutes' explanation about my work I found myself asking Ronnie to translate the following: "Ronnie, please tell this gentleman that his mother in spirit tells me he can discern colors." Ronnie was most taken aback and replied to me in English, "But Robert, this man is blind, and I know he has been blind since birth." I persisted and, being an excellent worker for Spirit, Ronnie translated word for word what I had said to the gentleman. "Of course I can," came the reply. Ronnie and I looked at each other in disbelief. How could this be, a man blind from birth could tell the difference in colors? We were both stunned, but he answered all my questions readily, even allowing us to "test" him.

We immediately got out various scarves and pieces of different-colored material, and one by one I handed him colored cloths. "Red," he called out, "this is what I call red," and it was red. Blue, green, yellow, purple— we tried them all, and even when I tried two whites in a row, he got it correct. I just had to know, how? This gentleman had a very gentle soul and told me that it was true he had never physically seen color, but as a child his mother would explain things to him, with great patience and love, letting him hold flowers and explaining that it was a red rose or yellow daffodil he was holding. Over the years he developed sensitivity to the vibrations that he claims colors give off—and that they actually do. How many of us use our eyes to see the beauty around us? Could you even close your eyes and discern color? How many things do we not actually see every day of our lives? These are the lessons taught to us by those souls who chose as a vehicle a body some see as less than "perfect." Despite the physical differences we are all the same, and the spirit can overcome any challenge.

RELIGION

I have already mentioned in Chapter 5 what Spirit explained to me occurs with the different religions after so-called death. At this point, when so much blame for many of the world's problems is leveled at religion, I think it is worth sharing further teachings from Spirit on the subject of religion.

As Ramadahn has pointed out, Spirit sees religions as "maps for this life," especially since the kernel of truth at the center of most of the world's religions is, "Do unto others as you wish others to do unto you." Man of course has added to, changed, and in some cases even twisted this simple truth throughout time to best suit his own ego, even going so far as to feel justified while doing so because he was doing it in the name of a preferred religion. But in order for religion to remain a map, it must be a useful guide, it should help the traveler to reach his destination. What if previous travelers took the long way around, or made mistakes, should we blindly follow them? I am told that while the core of religions should be the simple rule above, no religion should pointlessly restrict its followers and not allow them to grow as individual people or as a community. The point at which a religion starts dictating what is and is not allowed is the point at which that religion is ultimately doomed. Whether it takes years or thousands of years, if a religion is not open to spiritual growth in helping its travelers to understand others, then it is doomed to fail. Spirit has also pointed out that many of the problems surrounding religion today have come about because the various religious organizations have moved away from the very spirituality that first formed them.

The first problem that we encounter in all religions is that we tend to place priests, ministers, rabbis, mullahs, or any religious teachers or leaders on a pedestal, when the fact that we are all equal has been a fundamental spiritual teaching throughout history. We are then surprised when such people prove to be only human. Of course, we should expect shepherds to lead the flock, and they should lead by example. We do have the right to expect certain standards of our religious leaders, but when they show their human side, that should not be sufficient reason for us to abandon the religion entirely, especially if it is a faith that means something to us. Rather, we must focus on the important fact that it is the message, not the messenger, that is important. We should not place blind faith in our spiritual leaders, nor should we place our entire trust in

God in their hands. Spirit has told me that this is as true of religion as it is of mediumship.

Christianity has had a rough time during its history. It is easy to look at the different factions and point to what is wrong with them, forgetting that many Christian denominations have done good works all over the world. At the time of writing the Church of England has some of its lowest attendance ever, which is a shame, because I well remember the great orator Reverend Billy Graham preaching in London. I have to say this was one of the most spiritually inspiring orations I have heard and the church was standing room only. These days that same church would be fortunate to gather twenty souls to its Sunday service. The Catholic Church, throughout its history, has had problems, right back to its inception, yet people forget what great guidance, comfort, leadership, and good works it has achieved through its message. From the Inquisition, to assisting fugitive Nazis, to the present-day horrific scandal of child abuse, priests have been involved in some of history's blackest hours, but we must remember that no human is without sin. Many would think that after such a checkered history such an organization would be finished, yet Spirit has told me, through many sittings, where people have been urged to keep their faith, that there is much to be done via these religious organizations. I am told that the challenge being laid at the Vatican door is one that can help much of the world's population. That challenge is to lead man to a return to the essence of religion, to put aside the material quest and return to the spirituality they once taught. This spirituality must be taught by example.

It is of no surprise to me that in America three of the foremost respected mediums were either raised Catholic or are practicing Catholics. What does surprise me is that the Catholic Church has not spoken out about them. Could it be that the knowledge so long buried in the Vatican vaults is the same knowledge that these and many other mediums regularly demonstrate, that there is no death, and through the people known as mediums the so-called dead do communicate? To allow this knowledge to be widely known and not have control over these mediums would have meant the Church, as an organization, losing control of its adherents. I have asked this question of Spirit: Why has the Church never published its findings on mediumship? Each time I got the same answer. With or without the assistance of any religious organization, Spirit will continue in the pursuit of the goal to educate all people in the knowledge that there is life after death and that this can be demonstrated. I believe that as part of its own karmic cleansing, the Christian church now has many followers and members who are aware of the healing power of Spirit and who, now more than ever, desire to be shown the truth.

It is time for a return to spirituality for all religions, but in returning to that spirituality let us also be aware that Christianity was founded on facts, not faith.

Many people over the years have asked me, do I ever have any communication with such illumined souls as Jesus? I have to say I never have directly. But I have asked many questions of my helpers and guides, and the explanations that they have provided have helped me tremendously.

In my childhood reading the Bible was a joy. It was a book filled with miraculous stories, and I tended to just accept them as many people do. But over the years, I became confused with some accounts in the Bible. Much of what we believe about the man called Jesus involves events that occurred after his death. Would Christianity have survived these two thousand years if the events surrounding this man that took place after his crucifixion had not been recorded? I don't think it would have survived.

At his crucifixion, Jesus had been betrayed by one disciple, another had proven to be a traitor, and all the others had run away and hidden, at that very time when their leader needed them most. Christianity at that point had been thoroughly discredited. Not even the men who were the early followers believed in it anymore.

Yet it is the events after the so-called death of Jesus that led these same followers to become apostles and to continue to spread the word of the man who came to show the way. The fact that they saw their leader after his death, that from the life after this one, he appeared and gave proof of his continued survival, turned the disciples into zealous apostles. With the account of the meeting in the upper room, we have a clear recording that Jesus materialized to his disciples, that doubting Thomas was invited to actually touch him and thereby end any skepticism. From his first appearance to Mary Magdalene and from the many accounts thereafter, the Bible attests to the fact that the so-called dead survive physical death. It seems incredible that people who accept this teaching are often the first to condemn mediums. They often quote the Old Testament, sometimes Moses, saying that psychic phenomena are condemned. Yet if that is the case, Moses defied his own condemnation, for does it not also state in the Bible that Moses appeared with Elias and was seen talking with Jesus? Moses and Elias had, of course, apparently been dead for many years.

We hear that the disciples were not necessarily chosen for their education, their good characters or their calling. For the most part they were simple men in whom Jesus saw the potential of spiritual progress and the gift of mediumship. I believe the same is true today. The psychic gifts or mediumship potential are not always accompanied by intelligence, religious fervor, or social refinement. After the proof that Jesus continued to live, these twelve men were changed forever, in the same way that anyone having witnessed true evidence of the survival of their own loved ones is changed forever. The knowledge, comfort, and healing that accompany this realization is akin to what happened to Saul on the road to Damascus. And although Saul was what some may call a mercenary, after his psychic experience he became Paul the great champion of Christianity.

The evidence that I received from Spirit is that Christianity owes its very existence to the evidence supplied by psychic phenomena, and that if the effort was made to return to its true spiritual roots, the Christian Church has the ability to use this knowledge to furnish proof that there is no death. This can be demonstrated by the work done by mediums. I am in no doubt that the many whose calling is the ministry have the ability to develop their mediumistic gifts. If the Church followed such a path the world would be a more enlightened place. This is why I am told, by Spirit, that many people who are already members of various religions are being encouraged, prepared, and are indeed already demonstrating the gifts of mediumship. If the example comes from within the ranks, the truth cannot be ignored forever. I have already found that the better ministers, around the world and in all religions, exhibit signs of mediumship, clairvoyance, clairaudience, and healing. They are also the finest counselors.

I ask anyone to read again Chapter 12 of St. Paul's First Epistle to the Corinthians, where he lists the "spiritual gifts," and he makes the statement "of which I would not have you ignorant," and explain to me the difference between "discerning of spirits" and mediumship.

To make such suggestions as I have done took a lot of personal soul searching, and some may feel that I have deliberately attacked the failings of the Christian church. I do believe we have to put our own house in order first, but other religions have equally gone astray. It is a lack of understanding between the various religions that has caused so much pain in the world. If the Christian Church has strayed, others have in some cases completely missed their path.

The Holy Koran is as fine a map for the followers of Mohammed as any other book of spiritual guidance. In its pages we see many a familiar lesson, yet in the hands of a few fanatics it has been used to control a minority of its followers. Religious leaders who use their knowledge to encourage their followers to commit heinous deeds are truly evil, but anyone who gives over his or her free will to *any* other person has truly failed to comprehend the teachings of the great masters. When we hear of people being promised "paradise" by their leaders for committing evil acts, I can only recount the evidence I have received from the many sittings I have conducted, especially recently following the World Trade Center atrocity—there was no "paradise" for the perpetrators. In each case, they have had to stand before those they murdered and explain their actions, a most humbling experience, I am told.

One young victim of that evilness also posed the following question during a public demonstration of spirit communication I gave recently. "If the religious teachers, who peddle such nonsense of paradise for those willing to sacrifice their lives, really know this to be true, how come they are not so willing to do the act themselves?"

But I have to say that, traveling around the world as I do, I have found that Muslims who are peaceful, loving, and sincere are in the majority and that the wicked are a minority. Spirit's wish is that the house of Mohammed also gets itself in order and returns to the spirituality of its foundation. We are responsible as individuals and for each other.

The house of David never ceases to amaze me— such wisdom, such knowledge, such experience of all man's potential and of man's ability to plumb the depths of inhumanity. I have asked on many occasions why, throughout history, the Jews have been singled out for harsh treatment and defamation? Each time I have posed this question the answer came back the same. By being witness to such horrors, through experiencing such depravity, the house of David, with empathy and through the true application of the religion of Judaism, will one day lead the world to peace. This is their spiritual challenge, as it is for all of us.

Ramadahn has told me much about religion, but his assertion concerning all the different religions that "the test of any religion is the acceptance it preaches of other religions" is something that should be inscribed in every religious house.

PETS

As long as man has been around he has surrounded himself with companions from the animal kingdom. I have often been asked, "Do our pets also survive death?" I can categorically state, *Yes!* and I have witnessed the actual proof. In the first instance I have seen demonstrations by mediums in which they have linked all kinds of deceased pets with their former owners. Sometimes they accurately describe the animal, some are able to read the name tags on the animals' collars, and often the mediums are helped by their own guides and helpers in obtaining information about our pets. Our pets do not go through that transition we call death and suddenly through that process acquire the ability to speak English. They can, however, retain their ability to communicate.

A lady came to see me for a sitting; as usual I had no idea what her reasons or needs were. After some ten or fifteen minutes of my linking with various relations, I became aware of a dog in the room. I described the dog as best I could, whereupon the lady became visibly emotional, explaining that this was actually her reason for having the sitting. She just wanted to know that her canine companion was all right. Even after I had described the dog, his condition at passing, and his name, the sitter still just wanted to know that her dog was safe and at peace. This was the point when, in a short break in my talking, we both heard the unmistakable sound of a dog barking. Now let me explain the following: The sitting was being conducted in a room on the top floor of a hotel, no dogs are allowed, and I can assure you that I ran to the door to check the corridor. On returning from the door I asked the sitter, "Did you hear something?" "Yes," she replied, and pointed to the fact that during the whole time of our sitting, as in the case of all the sittings I give, the tape recorder was still recording. We stopped the tape, rewound it, and at exactly the point that I took a break from speaking, there was the clear sound of a dog barking. The unconditional love that this owner gave to her dog was, I believe, so perfect that Spirit decided to physically show her that her dog had indeed survived death. I believe my part was to provide the energy that some mediums have called ectoplasm, which I described earlier. This allowed the spirit helpers to produce a temporary spirit "voice box," which allowed us to hear that dog bark. I am terribly grateful to that sitter. Not only did she give me permission to tell others of our experience, she also copied the tape for me. It is, along with a ring from Lord Byron, a cross given to me by one of the world's finest mediums, and a silver bell used by Sir Arthur Conan Doyle in some séances, one of my most treasured possessions. The tape is a physical demonstration of the power of love and of Spirit.

To some people, losing a pet is the same as losing a child, and there is no point in saying, "Nonsense, losing a pet is not the same as losing your own child. As sad an event as losing a cherished dog is, how can we compare the two losses?"

We should keep in mind that there are many cases where childless couples or lonely people in particular have an animal that has taken the place of a child. In such cases, the love that is invested is the same and the loss of the physical presence is just as real as losing a child.

We can, I believe, learn a lot from the animal kingdom. In fact, I believe the animal kingdom to be one way that God allows us to learn the lesson of responsibility.

Domesticated animals such as dogs and cats have, over the years, provided the most evidence of their survival. Occasionally I have seen horses that I have been able to describe, including in one demonstration the blaze on the horse's head and its name (which appeared to me written on the blanket covering the horse). As is the case with mankind, where it is the individual consciousness that survives death, a consciousness that can show character and traits and has mental recall, so it is with our pets. It appears that a close association between humans and animals helps the animal to acquire or develop a distinct personality. Every animal lover will tell you that his or her pet had a personality. It is as if the love and care and friendship that we offer to such pets helps them to become almost "humanized." They in turn are often offering us a great lesson in unconditional love. Our pets through their close association with man develop some very human traits. They can express love and show intelligence, pleasure, dislike, and fear. They can develop a personality, and it is this that survives death. Through their close contact with humans they are able to show that they survive as individuals.

The key to all communication is love. There are only rare cases in which wild or undomesticated animals have returned as individuals, and in each of these cases such "wild" animals have always had some interaction with humans. Do we, the higher selves of all humans, possess the key for true evolution and progress? Have we not demonstrated by our love for our pets that unconditional love can help the animal kingdom? If that is the case then the animal kingdom is an example of how we humans should be treating one another.

REINCARNATION AND THE LAW OF KARMA

I feel that the evidence for man's survival after physical death as an intelligent, conscious individual has been well demonstrated and documented over many centuries, and I find this evidence to be incontrovertible.

But when I look at the subject of reincarnation I find myself in a quandary. In the first place, through all the thousands of spirit contacts I have had I found no evidence to prove that man reincarnates. By this I mean I have had no messages, information, or proof that any individual has been able to supply that cannot be contested by another explanation other than reincarnation. And yet I remain a firm believer in reincarnation.

Spirit has told me over and over again that we meet most people we have known on the Earth plane in the Spirit realms when we die. This means that people such as grandparents or even great-grandparents, indeed, in some cases, several generations, meet and are together in the spirit world. If this is the case, and we often get the evidence to prove that such people are in the spirit world, then clearly they could not have reincarnated.

The case for reincarnation is, though, a strong one. I found that where things go wrong is that people have taken a basic truth and distorted it. I cannot count the times I have met people who claim to have been Cleopatra or believe that they were some hailed pharaoh in a previous life. My standard answer to them is usually, "Get real, if everyone was such a person, who built those pyramids?" Often identifying with such an exalted soul is a panacea for a dreary current life. In recent times much has been done, by a few people, to peddle classes in which people can "discover" who they were. My problem with this is that we are, according to those who believe in reincarnation, a sum total of all that we have been. Clearly we cannot alter or change the past, so what is the point in identifying some distant character as us in another life? If it were for understanding that we had lived many lives to gain experience and for our soul to grow, this would indeed prove that we are eternal, and I would easily endorse this. But how do you *prove* that you have been another person? No one, to date, has offered me such proof. The accounts I have read are often inconclusive, with the possible exception of the Bloxham tapes. The Bloxham tapes were made by Arnold Bloxham, who audiotaped people while he put them in a hypnotic trance. In one case a woman undergoing hypnotic regression gave an account of a previous life that could not be confirmed until after an architectural dig that showed that the events she had described had actually occurred in the town. There is a possibility that the woman could have consciously or unconsciously acquired the knowledge from some recorded history of the event. But then she did recall a name that had been in no known records that was only revealed after the mud and dirt of hundreds of years were removed. There are many such experiences recorded.

But I feel that most such experiences as past lives could really fall into the déjà vu category.

Many of us have been to a place and on our first visit we *know* that we have been there before, yet in reality we can prove we have not. I have visited many cities on my travels, and I have had the experience of standing in a square or train station and knowing what I would find down a certain street. I have even known what type of stores or buildings I would find, and on more than one occasion I have even known what the next street would be named before ever seeing it. Now some would believe this may point to an experience in another life, but I think it only reinforces the accounts of astral travel. Astral travel, of course, occurs when we consciously or unconsciously visit different places without our physical bodies. It occurs when our beta body is able to emerge from the physical and journey afar. Often this occurs during the sleep state, and most people have no conscious memory of such events. A number of people have sought to promote astral travel by giving instruction on how it can be achieved. Considering that the beta is connected to the physical by only a fine silver cord, and this cord can easily be damaged by unexpected noise or shock, I do not recommend astral travel to anyone, other than the most experienced. I would recommend those interested in the subject read *Soul Traveler* by Albert Taylor. Each night we sleep, and we have so many accounts of people who describe astral travel that it would be hard these days to pass it off as flights of fancy. And I feel it is quite possible that most of us have engaged in astral travel—I certainly have stronger beliefs in the accounts of astral travel than I do in all the accounts of reincarnation.

Another reason I doubt that accounts of reincarnation are valid is that the accounts I have heard show that practically everyone who has made the transition we call death is not as anxious as you might think to return to this world. However, we do have this amazing thing called free will, and I do believe that it is this gift that allows some people to elect a voluntary reincarnation. Reincarnation, I believe, is not something that is automatic and compulsory but perhaps optional and left up to individual souls.

I have found that we do not undertake this or any journey in our lives lightly. It is my belief, based on accounts from those who have passed to the spirit realms, that before coming here we in fact write ourselves something akin to a "personal soul shopping list." Based on what we know our soul needs to experience, we can rely on our main spirit guide and other illumined souls who do their best to help us plan this list. When we are born we have no conscious memory of this list, but we have this wonderful gift of life, and the precious gift of free will. I also believe we have just enough energy for us to complete our list. These plans or lists do not state, "At twenty I must do this," or, "At thirty-five I must have achieved that," nor do they say I will have to complete everything by the age of fifteen or ninety. They consist of requirements for our soul's progression. It may be that we have made a list composed of love, jealousy, trust, truth, hate, or any number of different lessons in various combinations. When we start living this life it then affords us the opportunity to have experiences that teach us about such things, thereby educating our soul. Now as I said, we have free will, and some people choose not to learn from a certain experience. Most people even repeat the same lessons again and again in one lifetime. How many people do we hear of who escape from a marriage or partnership that seems hellish only to go directly into another that is similar? When we have had exposure to all on our list and we make that transition called death, it is then that we actually reunite with our guide and we receive our original list. We then have to honestly review our own lives and be responsible for the decisions we made. On our lists we may have many check marks to indicate that we had learned from an experience, and I am sure many of us will also have a number of crosses where we did not. What of the people who asked for the lesson of compassion? Perhaps on reviewing his life, a man might see that there was a time when he was asked to take care of Grandma, but for one reason or another, he decided that at the time he was too busy building his career or business. Perhaps he resolved his problem by placing the lady in a home and convincing himself that a once-a-month visit was justified. Could that person honestly review his life and say that he deserved a check mark for getting the lesson of compassion correct? It could be, of course, that he learned the lesson through another opportunity in his life, in which case, yes, he would have gotten it correct. It is my belief that it is only after a thorough and honest review of life that some might decide that they need to reincarnate and try to learn some lessons they had missed before. But we must see that as great as this Earth plane is, there are limits to what we can learn here. People who expound the theory that no sooner are we dead than we jump into another body are really mocking the whole process of life. I think some people see it as if mankind is like a hamster on a wheel. Running round and round, we get exhausted, die, and fall off the wheel, and as soon as you like we jump back on and start again. Does this not trivialize all that we go through? In fact I have also had sittings where an errant father has come through and apologized for his mistakes and then gone on to reveal that he had been watching a son or daughter to see how that person had dealt with certain issues. The father had also learned simply by observing other people in the situation he had been in and how they handled it—clearly he did not have to reincarnate to learn the lesson. So it is my contention that reincarnation is possible, and for some desirous, but it is not compulsory. Ramadahn, once again, came up with some advice for me. He told me that it is not important where or who we have been—that makes us what we are. What is far more important is who we are now and where we are heading. Fortunately, by getting to know our guides, and by listening to the higher self, we can change our direction in this life, we can get it right and at that time of reflection know that we accomplished all that we came here to do.

The Law of Karma is a true natural law, but it is widely misunderstood. Many people believe that karma is only about recompense and retribution. They use it to explain why some are born into poverty while others are showered in wealth. But that is a very selfish way of looking at karma. Like all natural laws, it is a simple one: If you fail to learn a required lesson when it presents itself to you, there is no escaping it. You will have to learn that lesson at some other point in your life. Which is why I learned that you can never run away from a problem. No matter how far you run you will meet the same problem at some other point in your life. Perhaps that problem will be in another guise, but meet it you will. So, when presented with a problem, the only thing to do is to stand and sort it out. Whatever the outcome may be, you will at least know that you dealt with a lesson and will not have to face it again. It is only a fool who refuses to learn any of the lessons while on the Earth plane; it is likely that these are the very people who feel the need to visit here time and time again. This has also led me to believe that the younger someone passes or the less time they choose to spend here the more truly evolved is that soul. I have to say that is why I feel I see souls who do not come to this life, such as miscarriages, as pure small white shining lights.

Just as the Law of Karma applies to the individual, it also applies to nations and to the whole of our planet. It is an immutable law, which means that individually and collectively we cannot escape the lessons that we need to learn. Which is why it is particularly frustrating when we make the same mistakes, when we have to yet again repeat the atrocities of war. Instead of reacting aggressively, should those who are truly inspired be saying, "Enough"? We have to stop thinking of ourselves just as individuals or nations, and start thinking about what we are contributing to the world, and the legacy we are truly leaving for those who have to use this classroom after us. The Law of Karma can be summed up by the saying, "the sins of the father will be visited upon the son." Do any of us truly want to leave a job that we can accomplish for someone else to finish?

CHAPTER 7

Life after Life

And as to you death, and you bitter hug of mortality, it is idle to try to alarm me.

—WALT WHITMAN

It is only natural that people wonder about what happens at that point that we call death. Where do we go? Is the idea of going into a white light real? Just where is the spirit world and what can we expect to find there? These are just a few of the questions that all mediums are, at some point, asked.

It has been my consistent experience through the sittings and demonstrations that I have given that the act of passing is of no great terror to the individual who is making their transition—no matter how they die. Of course it is of great importance and interest to those who remain on the Earth plane. I have had the privilege of sitting with a number of people during their passing from this world. Through the ability of clairvoyance, in all cases that I have witnessed, I have seen the beta body, or the soul, leave via the crown chakra or the top of the head. I have found no reason to believe there is any difference whether we are murdered or die through natural causes, whether it is an "accident" or suicide, a quick passing or one drawn out by a long illness. We all leave the physical body in the same way. Our spirit exits through the top of our heads and when the last connection to the physical body is severed, and the famed silver cord is cut, that is the exact point of so-called death.

Some people whom I have witnessed making their transition have been well and truly ready and prepared for their passing. In fact I have spoken with them psychically as they were passing and have even spoken with some spirits who had only been "dead" for a few minutes. So I cannot subscribe to the theory that we all need to go and rest or have a period where it is not possible to be contacted right after we pass. Of course some transitions are a shock both for the person dying and for those here on the Earth plane, even if the person passes in peace. It is totally understandable that for such people there is a period when they are subdued or cocooned, a period when they adjust to their new environment and accept the fact that they have withdrawn from the world of matter. At no time have I ever been informed by Spirit of any prescription or spiritual law whereby there is a generic rule that people have to wait two weeks or three months before they can contact us or us them. Although I have seen this written, I must say I am wary of any medium or spiritual teacher who feels the need to deal in absolutes. In the first instance we know that some people are bolder than others; some are even more spiritually progressed. So what is it that such people would have to wait for during these prescribed periods, some kind of celestial audition to see if they can communicate correctly?

It seems clear to me that having found that you have survived death, it is only natural that you would want to find a way to convey this to your loved ones as soon as possible. There are some very persistent characters here on the Earth plane—why would they suddenly become shy and docile at that point of death? Whatever the time frame is—whether it be moments or years after passing—the spirits will initiate the contact when they are ready. Some are more ready and will make contact more quickly than others. This is the simple truth as I have found it.

I also have little time for those who feel the need to try to identify with rigid pronouncements exactly where the spirit world is. The strangest pronouncement I have read is that the spirit world is three feet above the Earth plane. I remember reading this "fact" while flying at thirty thousand feet. I thought I should look out of the little airplane window to see what was below me. It is of little use trying to visualize the spirit realms through physical eyes. I can understand a medium trying to comfort bereaved relatives by attempting to give some explanation of where their loved ones are, but when one makes such absolute statements about where the spirit world is located, all one does is set limits, and it is only the world of matter that has limits. One of the best answers I have heard to "Where is the spirit world?" is, "Where is the Internet?" We cannot give the Internet a geographical location, but we *know* it exists. The same applies to the spirit realms. It is like unconditional love: We are inextricably bound to all we have shared unconditional love with, and true love knows no boundaries. The spirit world is all around us; we are part of it and it is part of us. Whether we realize it or not we are constantly interacting with it.

I have time and again had spirit communication whereby the person passing has described what it was like to have their loved ones with them at their transition. Some have spoken of the feeling of crossing a bridge. It seemed like for the first half of the bridge crossing they were well aware of those who remained on the Earth plane, walking across the bridge with them. Then someone who they knew who had died before them met them in the middle of the bridge for the rest of the crossing, leaving the Earth plane people behind. This is often the case with those who pass after a long illness or when they have been in a coma. This description is often given by spirits who have their relatives around them just before or at the point of death.

There have been many accounts of patients who have been unconscious for some time, but suddenly wake and announce that they "see" some long-dead relative. All too often this is put down to hallucinations brought on by medication. I have no doubt that our loved ones in the spirit world step forward to greet those who are soon to join them. When people die their beta body is free of the physical—as they approach death, the sluggishness that is the physical begins to have less weight impression on the beta. Therefore, as the beta begins to vibrate more quickly, they are able to perceive those who are already free from that heavy old overcoat we call a body. I am quite happy to accept that the nearer to their transition the more likely it is that they will see their loved ones who they thought were dead. I find it no coincidence that this often happens just before the passing. The shock of seeing someone who has already passed is so powerful that it could certainly stimulate the brain into a temporary awakening and bring somebody out of a coma. And of course the first thing such people would want to share is that they have seen someone they long thought of as dead. If you saw such a reality, wouldn't you want to tell those around you that "it's all right, if so and so is here, and there is no need to fear, for if they survived death, we will too"?

In the case of atrocities or multiple deaths (such as the World Trade Center attack), often it does take time for communication to come through, but again there are no set schedules. It depends on the character of the victim. Time is of the material, physical world; there is no time in the spirit world. What could be months here may be a blink of an eye there. The communication takes place when the spirit is ready. The medium may be prepared, the relatives may be desperate for news, but the communication will not happen if the person in Spirit is not ready. People in shock often need a period of reconciliation with what has occurred. This applies to the spirit world too.

In the case of the World Trade Center, some of the first experiences I had concerned some of the heroic firemen. This wasn't entirely surprising, since those who have often faced death are well equipped to make what appears to be a speedy return. To some degree, the constant danger they are exposed to makes them more aware of the fragility of this life. What has been interesting and consistent in the sittings I have given to various families is that the spirits communicating rarely announce directly that they were victims of this atrocity. To do so would alert the medium, and unless the medium lived on Mars, he or she could not help but be influenced by what he or she has seen or read in the media. In each case of the thirty or so families or relatives that I have worked with, the victims have spoken of their passing, describing how they recall walking in a human chain, hand in hand with many others. The help and love they received from those already in Spirit was unconditional. You see, people do not necessarily have to be advanced spiritually, but to some degree, the more accepting of the fact that the transition we call death will come, the more readily they can take such a transition in their stride. I found it no surprise that other spirits helped these firemen, who in turn helped the other victims. The firemen who have come across to me showed no fear, and some readily found ways to let their loved ones know they were okay directly—without the use of a medium. True to their character, they then helped others in their efforts to communicate.

It is interesting to speculate that we make great preparations for births in this life and hardly any for death, and yet it would appear that a death in this physical life is but a birth into the spirit world. I feel that those who accept so-called death as inevitable, and do not fear it, are invariably better equipped to communicate readily when that transition has occurred.

In the perfect order of things most of us want to be with our loved ones when they pass. I have spoken with many people who have lived in regret of "not being there" when their loved one passed into Spirit. It took a hard and personal lesson for me to comprehend that the spirit knows more than the physical self. This is a lesson I did not learn from any sitting or demonstration. It was the final physical lesson my mother showed me at her passing. I would like to share this experience as a demonstration of unconditional love of a mother for a son. It could equally apply to anyone who has regret at not being present when a relative passes through any situation.

It was in 1992 that my mother became ill. We did not know for sure what was wrong with her, as she refused all tests, but there was speculation that she had bronchitis—especially since she was a heavy smoker—but without the tests we could not know for sure. When my mother entered the hospital none of us five children thought she could be dying. One of my sisters did say to me, "If anything happens to Mum, I just couldn't be there, I wouldn't be able to stand it." I, on the other hand, was determined that I would be around should anything happen. It was very important to me that, if my mother were to die, I should be with her. After all—and my brother and sisters will not mind my saying this, since I was the baby of the family—I was, in many ways, my mother's favorite. About a week into my mother's stay in hospital, I had been in a church to conduct the evening service, and for some reason I had forgotten to take off the minister's badge that I used to wear. I approached the nursing station at the hospital as my mother had been moved from the bed I had last seen her in. I told the nurse that I had come to see Mrs. Brown. I did not realize it at the time, but the nurse took one look at my lapel badge and quietly said, "Ah yes, the lady in the last bed on the right." She then added, "About twelve days, sir."

Not realizing I was a relative, this nurse unwittingly told me that my mother was going to die. From that day on I was determined to be with my mother, and for twelve nights and days my siblings and I sat with her. I was alone with her on the twelfth morning, and it was 11:30. My mother woke, saw me there, and said, "This is ridiculous, look, I am all right, I have made it through the night, go home, you have things to do, I'll see you later." Reluctantly, I left at 11:35 A.M. At noon, just as my sister Jackie, the one who could not bear to witness my mother's passing, entered my mother's room, our mother peacefully passed to Spirit. I was at first very angry that I had not been there and was furious at the thought of being cheated out of this precious moment. How could it be that I, the so-called sensitive, had not felt or perceived what was about to happen? It took a long time before Ramadahn gently explained that my mother, the real her, her spirit, knew that her passing was imminent and that the parting was just as painful for her as it was for me. It was likely that she would not have left willingly had I been present and that to witness my mother's passing could have destroyed all I had come to believe. My sister, on the other hand, had needed to learn that physical death *is* a reality, which is why she had been chosen to reassure my mother. If this child who did not want to part from my mother could stand being there and survive, then the rest of us would be all right. Ramadahn further explained the simple truth to me: There were no good-byes, because there are no good-byes. I also learned never again to be someone who would say, "I wish I had."

I have also been informed on many occasions by Spirit that in that realm, thought is a reality. This could explain the many and differing accounts of what heaven or the spirit world is really like. Of the many accounts that I have heard, one description of the spirit world not only was very vivid but for the gentleman concerned proved later to be exactly what he had expected heaven to be. I was touring in Munich, Germany. I had finished a large public demonstration and was getting ready for bed in my hotel. Most unusually for me, I was aware of another presence in the room. I say unusually, because contrary to popular belief, most mediums do not go around twenty-four hours a day conversing with and seeing spirits. I was shown at a very early age the importance of closing down, lowering the vibration, and dealing with *this* life. My interest was such that at first I tried to ignore the other presence in the room. I even started to read a book. But try as I might, I would read a page and then realize that I had no idea what I had just read. I tried turning off the light and attempting sleep, since I had been so tired half an hour before, but now I could not sleep. Slowly, but very clearly, I saw an older man. First he was sitting in a chair opposite my bed, then he began pacing the room. I noticed that he had very little hair—in fact I felt he was almost bald. He also had large, distinct spectacles, was quite slim, and seemed very fit, walking backward and forward. It appeared that he was walking across the room, collecting something, then walking back across the room to look at something on the other side. He seemed friendly and quite excited. I was, naturally, curious about who he was and what he was doing, but of course I also wondered why he was there, since I certainly had not invited anyone to my room! I soon realized that he seemed oblivious of me. Whatever he was collecting from across the room, seemed to occupy all his attention. It really was a most strange scene, and I could not help but ask in my mind, "What are you doing?" He appeared to hear my thoughts and immediately became quite animated, "It's all in here, you know, just like I always said it would be." I had no clue what this meant and had no idea who this man was. I wondered what it was that he was looking at, and again he seemed to "hear" my thoughts. "It's the akashic records, they're all here, that's what I am dealing with now, do tell Ellie."

Now I have a little knowledge about what the akashic records are supposed to be: They are basically the sum total of every life, but I had no real interest in them and have not really even read much about them. But I did know someone called Ellie. In fact of the thousands of people that I have met, I know I have only ever met one Ellie, and that is Ellie Fristensky, one of the founders of the LOVE (Learning, Oneness, Victorious, Enlighten) center in Huntington, New York. The LOVE Center is a metaphysical center, which teaches and promotes spiritual truths. I also knew that Ellie lived in Memphis and that she was going to think it very strange to get a call from Germany from a medium who would be blabbering on about spirits in a hotel room talking about ancient and esoteric records. I tried to ignore this man, but his enthusiasm for these records was really infectious, and the more I tried to put things out of my head, the more I became aware of his thoughts, impressing my mind. After a while, I could stand it no longer: "Who are you, and what do you want?!" I almost cried out. In a split second this very busy man became sweetness itself. He explained that his name was Ellwood and asked would I please tell Ellie that all his work was correct. He also told me to tell Ellie to send love to D. He mentioned meeting Edgar and how they had talked and discussed so much. He described a massive hall, rather like a library, where he claimed he now happily read as much as he liked, and he claimed that he was helping to look after these books. After a short time he left. I didn't see him, but "felt" as if someone were still around.

Well, friends, I am sure you are wondering if I am crazy, and believe me I was thinking the same, but after about another hour of trying to get to sleep, I finally got out of bed and got dressed. The little hotel/pension that I was staying in did not have any telephones in the rooms; in fact, there were none for public use in the building, so at 3:00 A.M. German time I wandered out to a public telephone box, having dug out of my suitcase a bundle of business cards that I seem to collect on every trip. Fortunately, I had found Ellie Fristensky's number. With an intake of breath and feeling quite a fool I called Memphis.

"Ellie? This is Robert Brown. I am calling from Munich, Germany. You may think I am mad but something strange happened tonight in my hotel room."

Ellie just needs an opening like that! "Well lucky you, love!" came the reply.

"No, a man appeared, he said his name was Ellwood and that I was to tell you the following." Well, I relayed all the above, and bless her, she did not laugh at me. In fact it was clear that she was quite moved by what I was saying. Ellie took the time to explain that Ellwood Babbett was not only a dear friend of hers but also one of her tutors. He was a very well-respected sensitive, a mystic, and a man of great spiritual knowledge. Part of his work was to enter a trance state and explore the akashic records. Throughout his life he was in no doubt of their existence. His wife was D, Daria. He had been acquainted with and had quite a connection to Edgar Cayce, the great "sleeping prophet." This man Ellwood had lectured, demonstrated, and taught all and any who sought the truth that he had expounded here on the Earth plane. I was deeply honored that he chose me to communicate a message to Ellie and his loved ones. I never met him in this physical life, but I am glad that he found his truth and his heaven. I do hope one day to shake his hand.

I have witnessed other accounts of the spirit world, including men busy building houses for expected loved ones, people with beautiful gardens, children meeting grandparents and "growing up" in spirit. I am sure that a child's perception of his or her surroundings is different from a grownup's, and a scholar would have different requirements for heaven than a carpenter, and a homemaker would not necessarily find enjoyment in rolling fields or open spaces.

Interestingly enough, although the spirits speak of children "growing up" in the spirit world, whenever they appear in the sittings I conduct they always show themselves as they are physically remembered. This seems quite logical to me, since we probably wouldn't recognize their physical bodies at age thirty, though we would surely recognize the real them, their wonderful vibration. What I believe is meant by growing up is the maturing and education of the real you, which is why we continue to evolve even in the spirit world. We have tasks and lessons in the spirit world, and clearly they are not tasks that necessitate a material condition, but the world that we find ourselves in after passing is exactly as we choose to think it. There have been many different accounts of the spirit world (alone these could fill a book), yet I have never heard any communicator describe an ugly or horrible place, nor have I, in literally thousands of communications, ever heard anyone convey that they died too soon or that they were miserable in the place that they found themselves in. This is partly, I believe, because I have always tried to use my gift of mediumship to help others, and I attempt to use it to heal, therefore I do not attract the wicked, the evil, or those who are unprepared. I can see little point, in a spirit linking with a loved one on Earth, in telling them that they should not have passed when they did or that they are unhappy where they are. To me such cases point to the possibility that any medium doing such work is not fully developed and that the medium is not doing his or her work for the best of reasons, and therefore they are attracting spirits who are also not sufficiently advanced. This can be dangerous and of course is the root of the complaints often leveled at mediums by a few, who contend that we disturb or deal with evil.

This brings me to the question, so often raised, of what happens to evil people. I know some people who relish the thought that evil people are punished in some fiery hole or dungeon or are confined to an almost unimaginable hell. It seems odd to me that some adherents of all that is good can take an almost perverse pleasure in the thought of the suffering of others. If people are evil on the Earth plane, that is exactly how they arrive in the spirit realms. We do not go through this transition called death, pass through some pearly gates, collect a harp and a pair of wings, and suddenly become angels. The immutable spiritual law of like attracting like is very much in evidence at this point, and evil people will find themselves among their own. However, my guide Ramadahn has told me that progression is open to all; it is not something anyone can fake. Not even the most accomplished con man, fraudster, or evil person can thwart the hierarchy. Our spirit guides, who hold the blueprint of our lives that we wrote before our physical birth, wait patiently for such evil people to recognize their wrongdoing. This is not a simple process and some apparently make little if any progress. First, they have to review their acts—not only the way that they carried them out, but also their true motives, which are often personal greed or gratification. They then have to view the results of their actions. In the case of someone like Hitler, one can imagine that at some point in his reviewing his life, he probably put up what he perceived as a justifiable argument, perhaps insisting that he was only thinking of his own people. But sooner or later he would also be confronted with the horrors that resulted from his and his followers' actions. Such people escape nothing, I am told. They witness the results of their deeds and any spiritual progression necessitates their actually experiencing what each of their victims went through. When we think of some of the atrocities that some have committed, it is under-standable that we rarely hear of them again. For them to advance to the level that most genuine mediums wish to work on, evil people would have had to confront their actions, witness the reactions, actually experience their victims' torture and pain, show sincere remorse, and finally stand before those they harmed or did wrong to and ask their forgiveness. This is a process that is so dif-ficult, painful, and humbling, and so against the nega-tive character of the despots, mass murderers, or religious zealots who try to override man's free will, that it takes what we would count as many lifetimes for some to complete. What has been an eye-opener for me is that, I am told, when such a state of realization is reached, the victims invariably forgive their tormentors. The lessons of any evil actions should not, whether we are directly connected to them or not, be lost on the rest of us. We should also, I believe, begin the process of healing and forgiveness here on the Earth plane. The best example of this in recent years was given by the present pope when he forgave the man who tried to assassinate him.

I have met some people who claim to be involved and in contact with those who are evil. But often they are disillusioned souls looking for their fifteen minutes of fame, and invariably they end up regretting such quests. But make no mistake, like does attract like. That universal law operates here on Earth and in the spirit realms.

The majority of us will not come into contact with evil, and we will be met at that point of death by loved ones who have passed before us. We will recognize them, will be able to communicate with each other, and will realize the true and accurate statement that life goes on.

There are some very rare sensitives here on the Earth who devote their working lives to helping others who pass, those who cannot or have not realized that death has occurred. Perhaps the person who passed was very attached to some physical or material pleasure that he or she will not relinquish—or feels that there was something he or she still had to do. The sensitives who work on such cases are highly developed and often hold what are called "rescue circles." These are groups specifically formed to help lost souls find the light. These circles are strictly controlled, and the sensitives work closely with the spirit guides. I am suspicious of anyone who publicly announces that he or she does such work, since all true and sincere rescue workers do their work quietly and without fanfare. They never seek publicity and do their work solely for the love of humanity and the ultimate benefit that can come from all life progressing.

Chapter 8

Spirits All Around Us

I love you when you bow in your mosque, kneel in your temple, pray in your church. For you and I are sons of one religion, and that is the spirit.

—Kahlil Gibran

Though there are more mediums now than ever before, there have been people throughout all periods of history who we believe have been inspired by Spirit. The list is in fact endless. In every age there have been prophets or seers; in recent times some of these have been called mediums.

But in all lives Spirit plays a part. Some are aware of the influence of Spirit, others act through what they believe is a sense of justice or what is correct. There have, however, been many people who have truly been inspired. These range from great orators to scientists to those who have held public office. Some of these people have been well known while others we have never heard of. Well known or not, such people have one thing in common: No matter what their own personal agenda, their ultimate goal is the advancement of all life. Another sure sign that people are inspired by Spirit is that they rarely, if ever, seek gratitude or acknowledgment of their efforts. They have, of course, out of necessity, sometimes used their positions to bring attention to some injustice. But as a general rule people inspired by Spirit seek no personal gain.

Joan of Arc, one of the most remarkable women of all time, believed at the age of thirteen that she heard "voices." She believed these voices to be those of St. Margaret, St. Catherine, and St. Michael urging her to free France from English rule. Such was her belief in these voices that she rallied her countrymen, withstood ecclesiastical examination, and was allowed to enter Orléans with an advance guard and within two weeks had forced the English to retire, thereby ending what amounted to the occupation of France by the English forever. Her belief in her mission and the voices cost her dearly, and she became one of the first in history to die for the ill-conceived concept of nationalism. However, her spirit inspirers or voices proved that no man should be subject to the domination of another, as indicated by her remarkable triumphs. To the end of her physical life Joan remained faithful to the "voices" and was burned at the stake and became a martyr. She was canonized by the Catholic Church in 1920.

As I have said, the list is endless: Abraham Lincoln, who attended séances, Martin Luther King, Jr., Nelson

Mandela, Mother Teresa of Calcutta, Sir Winston Churchill, Emily Pankhurst, Mahalia Jackson, Walt Whitman, John F. Kennedy, and one of my personal favorites of recent times, Maya Angelou, are all people who are among the many that I believe have been inspired by Spirit to help their fellow man. Also, if you listen to the songs sung by John Denver and pay attention to the words—can you doubt that he was truly inspired?

One person who I know was, at times, inspired by Spirit was Diana, Princess of Wales. The princess had several sittings with me and, as I stated earlier, I will never reveal the contents of any sitting and those with the Princess will be no exception. I did find it rather sad and a little strange that the princess never wanted to take any of the three audiotapes of her sittings with her when she left our meetings, providing instead an envelope for the tape to be posted to her after she left. When it was received she would have sent a little "official" Kensington Palace thank-you card to confirm that she had received the tape. In the light of recent allegations, I am glad that I did not keep any of the tapes but did retain the thank-you cards. The princess, who must have met thousands of people, seemed to be a rather lonely person. The former nun who introduced us, and who was also one of the instigators of the princess's meeting Mother Teresa, does not want to be named, but I believe even this kind lady was inspired by Spirit to effect such a meeting. In a very brief moment, outside our sitting, I dared to ask the princess which person she admired most. I was surprised that she mentioned a well-known singer and entertainer, saying rather wistfully, "I admire anyone who has the guts to turn their life around."

Spirits are around all of us. Some, like those listed above, consciously or unconsciously allow the very highest to work with them and through them. This is something that is open to all of us. I have been told by spirit communicators that it makes no difference to them who a person is or what their position in life is. We can all profit from taking the time to "listen" and follow the direction of Spirit. I am sure that many people will be thinking, "Well, I am not a princess, a writer, a campaigner, or a politician, what can I do?" The truth is that all of us can benefit ourselves and the world around us by being open to Spirit. It is interesting that many people who are Spirit-inspired have witnessed great hardship or have led troubled lives or have seen man's inhumanity to man.

My friend Steve is such a person, a veteran of Vietnam and a successful businessman. Steve knows me well. His wife and daughter first came to see me some years ago, and at first they did not think Steve would want a sitting, since his father is a minister and he was born and raised in the good old South. But Steve has had many psychic experiences, and I asked him once how he thought such experiences had helped him in his life. In a candid moment, he told me that they had helped him to form his own approach to life, and to this day he tries to do at least twelve things a day for another person. His one rule is that if the person being helped finds out who has helped them, then it doesn't count as one of his "good deeds of the day." I think this is a wonderful way to live. The children's song, "If everyone lit just one little candle, what a bright world this would be," comes to mind. Steve's life is a wonderful example of how all of our lives can be inspired by Spirit.

When I tell people that our spirit friends and loved ones are all around us, it concerns some people. "Are they watching us all the time?" "Do they just follow us around all day?" are questions that are often put to me. Our loved ones, guides, and helpers in the spirit world have purpose; their souls are still progressing. They do not "snoop" on us nor do they invade our privacy. Ramadahn once explained that it is something like being at a party or a gathering. You may go to a party with your wife or partner where you physically separate, probably meeting different people and discussing different things. All the time, though, you are aware of your partner's presence at the party. When it is time for you to connect one or the other will send a glance or attract the other's attention, and you'll come together. Spirit communication works the same way. If you feel the need to contact a spirit or the spirit feels the need to contact you, one or the other can send a sign or signal. For those of us in the physical body trying to get into contact with a spirit, it is often sufficient for us to just think of the person, to simply inquire "how they are." We do not—and should not—have to plead or beseech. Nor should we ever demand that a spirit come to us. I have pointed out to people, when they have come to me insisting that I get so-and-so in the spirit world, that insisting somebody do something rarely works in this world—why should it work in the spirit world?

We do not always need the services of a medium to receive spirit communication, but it is sometimes difficult to be objective when we are dealing with people we know and love. It does sometimes require a medium to help recognize the signs that a spirit is around—sometimes the signs are already there and quite obvious, but sometimes a medium is necessary to just point them out. I have been asked whether those who have passed ever return in another guise. For example, one lady told me that after a relative's passing, she often saw butterflies, and for a while she wondered if there was any significance in this. First of all, I do not believe in coincidences, but neither do I believe that our loved ones return in another form. However, I do know that spirits do send signs. In this case the sign of a butterfly was significant to the person concerned, and it is interesting that, as a symbol, the butterfly denotes transformation. The woman who asked me this question is very fortunate, as whenever she is questioning or un-sure of something, invariably she sees a butterfly and knows instantly that her loved ones are near.

Many of us will not be content with signs or sym-bols, but it is not possible for most people to be still and not focus on this world for even a short time. Such people are still surprised that they cannot see or wit-ness their loved ones in spirit, yet it is only when we shift our focus, mentally, spiritually, and emotionally, away from the cares of this world that we can even begin to glimpse Spirit and the spirit realms. Until we can learn to do that and make a true connection with people in spirit, we may have to settle for some of the most common signs that our loved ones are around. Some of the most common signs are:

Lights flickering. I would never just accept that if a light flickered once or twice, this was a sign from Spirit. But I have witnessed Spirit interacting with this world via electricity. This should hardly be surprising, as elec-tricity is something we all know vibrates quickly. I think this is one of the most common phenomena. One of the most impressive such signs that I have witnessed happened at a hotel I stay at in New York. In the room was a television housed in a wooden cabinet. Of course, when people visit me, the television is off and the cab-inet is closed. On numerous occasions, especially, it seems, when there was a young person with whom we were seeking to communicate, the television would suddenly turn on. The first time this occurred I thought that someone had sat on the remote. After the people had left, I tried turning the television on via the remote, with the wooden doors closed, and it would not happen. When this kept happening, I began to hide the remote in the other room, and still the television would come on. Even after the hotel had checked the electricity and changed the television, occasionally the television still turned on. What I have noticed is that when such a strong sign as this occurs, it is invariably when the atmosphere is charged, and usually for some reason the communicating spirit is young or very strong.

Scents. Occasionally, people will smell a scent that they immediately associate with a loved one who has passed. When this happens several times and in different places, you can be sure that person is around.

I would not expect people to accept any and all happenings as a sign from Spirit, but some are fortunate enough to be told to look for certain gifts or proofs—the moving of a mirror or photograph, for example. If you see that a mirror or a piece of furniture moves, it could be a signal from Spirit. If this happens once or twice, it is probably just a member of the family, but if you find that you are continually walking past a frame or mirror and straightening it, and you do not live in an earthquake zone or have a clumsy housekeeper, perhaps you should be considering how else it could move.

Gifts. Gifts, in the form of feathers, shells, coins, or wind chimes that sound when they are not outside and not in an obvious wind can also be signs that your loved ones in Spirit are seeking ways of letting you know that they are around.

Visitation. One of the strongest signs is the visitation, which is quite different from a dream. Often visitations are misinterpreted. People have told me that they have "dreamed" of their mother or father, and that it seemed real, but then for some reason they felt or saw their loved one crying. On awakening this can be quite distressing, because we feel something has happened but we do not like the idea of our loved ones being sad or upset. So we will often dismiss these visitations. A dream to me can be vivid, but usually they are senseless, and often we can explain them rationally. But visitations are quite different. They are rarely long in duration but are always very real. When I have asked people about these visitations, nearly all find it almost impossible to explain what it is that makes them so real and vivid. My friend Lilia Logette had a visitation during which her deceased father actually held her hand. A visitation usually occurs when we least expect it, when we are emotionally drained. To be in the altered state that a medium enters, we have to let go of our inhibitions, prejudices, and fears. This is not easy for most people, but when we are emotionally drained, when we are tired or exhausted, often these things just do not seem important, and we are more open to spirit communication. So, it should be no surprise that this often happens during our sleep time, when we are most open. Sometimes someone will wake during such a visitation and be absolutely sure that someone is in the room. But more often the visitation is very simple and very real—a common experience is the touching, holding, or caressing of a loved one. Often there is something said, but even if this does not happen, these meetings are always emotional, and that is why sometimes on awakening we think our loved ones were in distress. But that is only our mind's association with death. In actual fact these tears are tears of joy at the reunion.

These visitations are often experienced at night when we are asleep, but I have been fortunate enough to have a personal experience of one of these visitations that occurred in broad daylight, which I will recount later. In the meantime, for those of you who are seeking to connect with your own loved ones, I will share this Spirit-inspired poem for you to reflect on.

Spirits All Around Us

Think of me when sleep is near
And I who love you am so far away,
Think of me then and I'll come to you
Nor leave you 'til night turns into day.

Stretch forth your hand and in the depths of night
Another hand will grasp your fingertips,
And as of old you'll hear my voice
As I lightly press a kiss upon your sleeping lips.

—Spirit-inspired author, anonymous

Chapter 9

Sean

Courage is the price that Life exacts for granting peace.
—Amelia Earhart

I said in the last chapter that I would share my experience of a visitation. I do not believe it is because I am a medium that I was able to witness this, because I have had many people describe similar accounts of actually seeing or meeting with someone after that person has passed. Often this occurs during the night or when we are asleep. But my experience occurred during broad daylight, and I believe it occurred because of several factors, not least of which was the close bond between myself and the person concerned. It may also have happened because our friendship never really made "sense," and the person concerned was learning from me but also had come to teach me. It is also clear that shock played a part on both sides. I believe this example goes to show why some people are in our lives.

I met Sean in 1992. From the beginning most of my Spiritualist friends did not care for him, and some of my friends who are mediums positively disliked him. At first meeting though, most people thought he was "fun." He was very different from my usual friends. He was extremely outgoing, to the point that you could leave Sean anywhere for five minutes and by the time you returned he would have a group of people around him. He was humorous, and was great at telling anecdotes, for he had packed much into his thirty-two years. He had trained as an actor, appearing at the national theater, was passionate about sports, especially soccer, and was good-looking to the point that people would sometimes stop and stare at him, and more than once at a bar some girl would slip her telephone number to him. He was a free spirit in the sense that he hated making plans—so if you did manage to get him to agree to a meeting, you never really knew when, or if, he would turn up. Often, who he met that he found interesting along the way dictated whether he would turn up alone or with people, and rarely if ever was he on time. He appealed to both men and women, in that he could converse with both freely on most subjects. But there was a dark side to Sean: Not only was he an inveterate smoker, he was also an alcoholic. I was not aware of this at our first meeting, although on reflection I recall he was hopelessly drunk and quite rude. At the time, I just thought he was someone who had had one drink too many. What famous words those were to become.

Sean fascinated me, and somehow I felt responsible for him. Sober, he was intelligent, witty, kind to those in need. How often we would be walking down a road chatting away when suddenly I realized that Sean was no longer by my side. When I turned to look for him, I would invariably find he had crossed the road without any warning to help some woman with a wheelchair off the bus. Many was the time he disappeared across a street and I would find him giving his last coins to some beggar or homeless person. Given the financially pre-carious nature of his work as an actor, I would always say, "Why have you given your last money away, now you will not have any yourself?"

"That's all right," he would say. "I can always get more; these people have nothing." He was very vulner-able, and his main concern in life was that his mother and younger brother were okay. He was very protective of them both. Whenever things got too much for him, Sean would go on a "bender." I have never seen any-one before or since who could drink eighteen pints of Guinness in one session. After his drinking bouts Sean would be in a reflective mood, and his questions about the purpose of life were endless. He had been raised a Catholic, and it was after his friend's death from a drug overdose that he began to consider what happens when we die. Unbeknownst to me at the time, he had been visiting priests asking them what became of us and if there was anything to fear at that point of death. Later he was to tell me that none of them could give him what he felt was an acceptable answer. Occasionally, he would drop by my apartment or, if I was seeing clients, I would find him outside waiting for me. On one such visit I had just seen a cantor from the synagogue and his family. It had been a very successful sitting and I know that the client in question left very happy with what he had heard from his young son in Spirit. I was unaware that Sean was outside, and a few minutes after my clients had left, the doorbell rang. It was Sean. A strange conversation followed. He sat down and suddenly said, "You know, I have known you five years. I don't really know what you do nor how you do it, but I have watched people who visit you, and all I can say is that the ones I have seen certainly leave a lot happier than when they arrive, so it must be a good thing."

He asked me then to do a sitting for him and to try to contact his friend who had died of an overdose. I explained that this would be difficult, because I knew almost everything about Sean and his friends. I had sat through many a drunken confession about who was who and what each meant to each other, so it would be difficult for me to give an "objective" reading. I would probably interpret Spirit's message too much. I told Sean that in my opinion, if he asked, simply asked his friend in spirit to show himself in some way, then that person would find a way to contact him, provided that they were real friends. Another reason I did not want to do the sitting was that I felt that no matter what evidence I came up with, Sean would probably believe I had at some time been told this by him, possibly while he was in a stupor. I felt he needed his own experience. I had no idea whether what I suggested would help.

At eleven in the morning, one day, I happened to telephone Sean and there was no reply. This did not bother me, for I knew that when he was not working or if he had been partying the night before it was usual for him not to surface before noon. Just after midday my telephone rang, and it was Sean.

"Did you call me about an hour ago?"

"Yes," I replied. "If you heard the phone, why didn't you answer?"

He told me that he had heard the telephone and, in fact, knew that it was me calling. Well, of course, this annoyed me. "So why didn't you answer?"

"Well, I was having this dream, except I wasn't really asleep. I heard the telephone, I somehow knew it was you, but the dream I was having was so nice." He explained that he had been asking for a sign from his deceased friend Terry for months.

In this dream he said that he had seen a ship, and on board this ship there were people who he knew instinctively were all "dead." I asked him the details.

"I walked onto this ship and there was Terry standing by the rail. I walked up to him and said, 'Hello Terry, how are you?'

"He turned and said, 'Sean, I'm not dead,' and then he touched my arm, it was fantastic."

"That's it?" I almost screamed down the telephone. "He said he was not dead and then you thought you touched him? That's all it took for you to think something was 'fantastic'? What did that do for you?" Sean replied, "You don't understand, I actually touched him and the way he told me that he was 'not dead'—well I am no longer afraid of death anymore." Sean never mentioned this visitation again.

Three months later, after a trip to the south coast of England with our friends Heather and Antoinette, the four of us were traveling back on a train to London, all of us exhausted from the excesses of the weekend, having been to parties and meeting up with old friends. Heather, Antoinette, Sean, and I had all known each other since 1992. In fact, both of the girls had been attending the mediumship development classes that I used to run at my local church. Heather was using up the film in a disposable camera she had with her and was taking pictures on the train. We arrived in London and Sean and I headed off to the west of London while the girls went their way. We arrived at my flat around 3:30 in the afternoon. Sean decided to leave to visit his mother at 4:45. I had a demonstration booked at a church that evening, so when Sean suggested going for a drink at a local pub, I declined, and he left, saying, "If I don't call you tonight, I will speak to you tomorrow." Ten minutes later I was getting my suit and clothes ready for the evening's demonstration, and for some reason I could not find the minister's badge that I used to wear. I felt the urge to call the local pub to see if Sean had picked it up or was pulling some prank. When I called, another friend, Michael, answered, and when I asked for Sean, Michael replied, somewhat in a panic, "Oh, he just left," and the telephone went dead. Less than five minutes later Michael was at my door, and the poor man was absolutely distraught. Sean had apparently walked into the pub, ordered a glass of water and a pint of Guinness, drunk the water, taken two steps back, and collapsed. An ambulance had been called and they had taken Sean to the hospital. Immediately I asked Michael to call the church and cancel my demonstration. I ran around to Sean's mother's house. It seems strange now how things unfolded, but just outside his mother's house was another friend, Adrian, who was working on a car. Adrian did not live in that street, and yet here he was right outside Sean's house. I collected Sean's mother and asked Adrian if the car was working. When he said yes, I asked him to get us to the local hospital, where the ambulance had taken Sean. On arrival, I knew immediately that things were not good. Some of the staff at our local hospital know me, and they averted their eyes the moment I walked in. It took a few moments for the nurse to explain that Sean had collapsed and had stopped breathing. It had been a massive heart attack and nothing could have been done to save him. In fact, I later learned that he had actually passed while in Michael's arms, but the first thought Michael, a sensitive person who has known me for almost thirty years, had was, How is this going to affect Robert? and he could not bring himself to tell me the bad news. To this day I am grateful that Michael was there for Sean.

That evening passed in a kind of fog. At first I felt the need to comfort Sean's mother, and then I helped his brother with the police and the formalities at the hospital. Later that evening I fell into a deep sleep. I am sure I was in shock. The next day around 11:00 A.M. I awoke and realized that both Heather and Michael were in my living room. They had both stayed the night at my apartment, and I could clearly hear them talking. I heard Michael say, "I think this could destroy him and all that he has come to believe. I hope he can get over this." It was just at this point that, fully awake, conscious of the conversation going on in the next room, I felt my eyes drawn toward my bedroom door, where steadily but very quickly an image appeared. I saw Sean. It was no trick of the imagination: He was there. He stood in the doorway and said, "Have you got any money? I need to get some cigarettes."

Such was my shock and wonder that I replied, "Yes, there is ten pounds in my trouser pockets on the chair over there." Sean moved and went back to the door, at which point I thought, "You don't need that much for cigarettes, you're going for a drink, I'll come with you." Instantly I heard Sean say, "No, you cannot come this time," and in a second he was gone. It was so clearly him. That is how very real and comforting, how unmistakable a visitation is. They are simple and true.

Several of us have had many signs from Sean, some of them as irreverent as he sometimes was. I recall, a year after his passing, as I was visiting his grave, I thought it would be a nice gesture for his mother to see that someone had placed candles at his headstone. I was mindful of the family's Catholic beliefs and obtained candles contained in glass, the kind that often have the Virgin Mary pictured on the container. No matter how many times Heather and I tried to light those candles they always went out, and it got to the point where we ended up in a heap of laughter at the grave. Not to be outdone, I even got perpetual candles, ones that, if they are blown out, relight themselves. They never stayed alight either. We knew that Sean was somehow involved in that. Another convincing sign came but a few weeks after Sean's funeral. Heather developed the film from the disposable camera that she had used on the train some three hours before Sean's passing. Nothing about them seemed too extraordinary at first glance, except that Sean and I were sitting together, and around me there appeared sunlight. Around Sean there seemed to be a brown cloud or mist. I asked Lionel Owen, the former president of the International Spiritualist Federation, to look at the photos but gave him no other information. Lionel is very interested in psychic photography and is quite knowledgeable on the subject. The second he received the picture, he immediately pointed to Sean and said, "This person must have passed, what you have captured here is the last of his energy." It was very comforting for us all to know that Sean, despite being only thirty-nine, had not "passed before his time," that he had completed what he came here to find and share. It was only while doing a private memorial service for Sean that the penny finally dropped, when I was recounting some of the things that had occurred in the six years we had been friends. I had been asking, "Well, what was that all about, how come such a person entered my life and had so swiftly left?" I realized immediately that it was easy to stand in a pulpit and tell people what they should be doing and then blithely go about one's own business, not putting such advice into practice. If meeting me had helped Sean not to fear death, my meeting him showed me that many of us talk about good deeds, many of us think we are better because of our work, education, or calling. It took a vulnerable victim of drink to show me that if we are going to espouse spiritual goodwill we should also be willing to carry it through in our actions.

CHAPTER 10

So What Can
Spirit Communication Do for Us?

To know the road ahead, ask those coming back.
—CHINESE PROVERB

I have come to the conclusion that communicating with Spirit is not for everyone. Some people do not desire it, others are opposed to it, and some, on both sides of life, are simply not ready for it. With my mediumship I have always wanted to be better with each communication, and I don't think I will ever be satisfied with the results, for I am always trying to push the known boundaries.

I often meet people who, no matter what information mediums relay from Spirit, always try to rationalize, saying at worst that they obtain information beforehand or at best that we somehow read people's minds. Every time one of these objections has been raised I have always turned to Ramadahn to ask if there was some way that we could demonstrate that such explanations were complete fabrication. He has always found a way. In the first place, one look at my calendar and even a cynic would know that at the rate that I travel, I could never hope to obtain information on so many people in so many different countries. It is not uncommon for me to visit ten countries in one year. Also, I would have to employ an army of informers to gather such information, and I can assure you, I do not. When I agree to do public demonstrations I have no control over who attends, and the messages are random. Even I do not know until I stand up where in the room I will be directed to. I have always been directed by Spirit where to go. I am not in favor of mediums who stand and say to a packed hall, "Does anyone here know a 'John'?" In any hall a number of people will know most names.

I have seen the difference that true communication can make to someone's life. It does not have to be that the person has been directly affected by the death of a close relative; a case in point happened in March 2002. I was asked to give a sitting to a friend of my friend Steve. Curiously enough, when I was introduced to this man, I was told only that this guy's name was also Steve. He seemed a nice fellow, but there was something about him that appeared "broken." He seemed a little wary of me, and once we were left alone and I had switched the tape recorder on, he immediately asked me to verify whether in fact I knew who he was. I replied that I had no idea who he was. This man seemed so drained he looked young middle-aged, but something about him gave off an air of having been "beaten up" or having gone through a mangle. He seemed to be defeated, and yet he had the look of someone who would not give up. We spent almost one and a half hours in that sitting, and most of the time that I was relaying information, "Steve" would either nod or grunt yes or no to what I said. He never gave one shred of information. It was as if he were a professional listener. He said, "Okay, tell me what you see or hear." The information that came through was precise, horrific, and extremely detailed. When we finally finished, I asked "Steve" if he wanted to join the rest of us downstairs, but he said he wanted to be alone for a few minutes. After a while, he joined the rest of us in my friend's family room. He was carrying a large envelope, and once again he asked me in front of my friends whether I had any idea who he was. At this point even my friends chimed in, "Steve, Robert lives in London, he has no idea who you are." At which point he handed me the envelope and said he would like to give me a present. Inside was a book. The inscription read "To my incredible new friend Robert, you are remarkable! With kind regards Steve Thomas." The book was *Jon Benet, Inside the Ramsey Murder Investigation*, from a leading detective on the case, STEVE THOMAS, with Don Davis. Such was the information that came through that I saw a visible change in this man. He seemed to have regained his strength, and when he departed it was as if a dark, heavy cloud had lifted from his shoulders.

Another claim laid at mediums' feet is that we do "cold readings." Much has been said in the media about "cold readings." Skeptics point to the fact that many mediums ask questions in a veiled way. For example, "I have a man, connecting from Spirit, he seems to be like a father, is your father passed?" When the sitter answers yes, the medium is then working on information given by the sitter, not directly by Spirit. Also, in a cold reading, often many names are thrown out at the sitter ("Do you know a Bob? A John? A Michael?"). Of course, the ones that mean something are acknowledged, and the ones that do not fit are quickly passed over. I am sure that some unscrupulous people do such things, and I have reviewed some videotapes where it was clear that, far from giving evidence, some people have engaged in a kind of question-and-answer, hit-or-miss kind of game. I blame not only the mediums but also the people who push such mediums. There is a hunger for information, a desire to know and believe, but instead of making sensational claims for instant gratification, why are we not investigating properly? It should be obvious to all in search of the truth, including mediums who value their integrity, that the less a medium knows, the better!

One of the things that I was asked long ago by someone in an audience was "Are you reading minds or is there something to this?" whereupon I was immediately aware of Ramadahn's presence. He told me to say the following: "If I can tell you what is on your mind and then something that you cannot know but something that could later be verified, would that at least keep your mind open to the possibility that I am in contact with someone other than your mind?" I repeated this and the person agreed that he was willing to try. I went on to tell him he was worrying about his job, that he felt he was going to get fired, and a few other things that he agreed were troubling him. Then I went on to describe his father, who was in Spirit. I told this man that he had his father's watch, and he agreed that it was somewhere at home. I told him that the watch worked, but was not running, and he replied that he thought that probable, but he had not seen it for some years. I further conveyed that it was in a drawer in his bedroom, and again he thought that it could be. Then I relayed that once he located it he would find that the watch had stopped at eighteen minutes past the hour. Of course it sounded impressive, but equally it could not be proved there and then. What I did not know was that the man in the audience lived very close to the hall, and during the fifteen-minute break he went with two other people from the audience to his house. They located the watch, and it was at the exact time that his father had said. Ramadahn had found a way to prove that we do not read people's minds, for even a cynic must admit that you cannot read what is not there. I am still unsure if anyone can read another's mind. Certainly telepathy is a reality, but that requires two consenting minds, a transmitter and a receiver. Was Ramadahn relaying what was in the man's mind? Was I picking it up from the man's aura? Whatever the case, the watch was something that was not part of any of this man's knowledge, and that information had to come from somewhere. I have had the good fortune to repeat this kind of demonstration on numerous occasions, in different countries around the world.

Apart from obtaining information, spirit communication can and does remove the fear of death, and in its truest form this is the greatest truth known to mankind. It can and does transform lives, and I believe with the right training and guidance it can help to heal the world. We do have a problem with our mediums. I know that, with the increasing popularity of mediumship on television, whenever there is an offer of a workshop or class on the development of mediumship we are inundated with people who want to learn. They are often surprised when I start such a day with, "Please do not think you will leave here today knowing everything about mediumship, the reason being, I do not know everything, so therefore I cannot teach you everything." I have found the gift of mediumship to be like an onion. Each time you peel one layer there is another. I also do know that mediumship is rather like the surgeon's scalpel: In the hands of the trained it can create near miracles and in those of the untrained it can make a bloody mess.

I have also been told by spirit communicators that there are individuals and whole groups of people on the other side who are waiting patiently to work with us, to share newfound knowledge that will help and assist the Earth in as many ways as we can imagine. They assure me that information, knowledge, and answers are available to those who seek in earnest, but that we have to show that we are deserving of such trust.

The Appendix that follows is an aid for those wishing to learn about mediumship and its development, so for now I will say . . . The end—or is it the beginning?

PART THREE

APPENDIX

Fail to prepare, prepare to fail.
—Advice on mediumship from Ramadahn, my spirit guide

I have heard many a medium tell inquirers, "it just comes naturally," or, "I was born psychic, I never had any training." I know this to be true in many cases, but for a long time I wondered if there was anything any of us could do to make ourselves better instruments for Spirit to work with. Over a period of time Ramadahn, the spirit guide who has been a blessing to me, has patiently pointed out faults, corrected mistakes, criticized, and given direction on how I could improve the instrument known as Robert Brown. It is, I found, a never-ending quest. One of the first acknowledgments we all have to make is that none of us are perfect. Part of our very reason for being is that we are being given a fantastic opportunity, called life, to improve, enhance, and educate the real us. This holds true for all forms of life.

Mediums' first hard lesson is to accept the fact that they alone do nothing. Their only source of information is the cooperation that they have with the spirit world. Over the years many a gifted medium has made the fatal mistake of believing that the messenger is more important than the message, and Ramadahn made a point of telling me that ego has been the spiritual death of many a fine instrument. In my own lifetime I have seen fantastic mediums, and a few have made the mistake of believing that they alone are the salvation of man or they have begun to believe the sycophants who sometimes surround them, telling them how great they are. In all such cases, it is inevitable that sooner or later the gift that made them known is no longer evident. I have heard many an old-time medium say, "If you abuse your gift it will be taken from you." There is some truth in this, but it was explained to me by Spirit that in all cases it is the instrument who moves away from the source: Our spirit helpers will never desert us. Our spirit guides stoically hold their position, which is built on truth. If any medium abuses or misuses that truth, it is the medium, using free will, who is moving away from Spirit. Our guides and helpers can only watch with sadness and anguish and hope that we will use our free will to return to the right path. Free will is just that, there are no strings. We can exercise our free will, but we must also accept the consequences of our decisions.

One of the first questions all potential mediums should ask themselves is, "Why do I want to do this?" If the answer, the true answer, is anything other than, "I want to help others," Spirit's advice is to not even start your mediumistic development, for you will be building on shifting sands.

Having decided that we wish to help others and ergo improve our real selves, we need to present to Spirit a vessel as untainted as possible, which spirits can use to fill with their love, wisdom, and guidance. Now let us not be naïve here: There is not a person walking this Earth who has not acquired some prejudices, inhibitions, or fears during their lifetime, but in mediumship such things have to be put aside, if only temporarily. One of the reasons that mediums cannot function all the time in "receptive" mode is that at some points they have to be their physical selves. How many times have people been in awe of a speaker, politician, church leader, or medium only to find at some time that same person has another side to his or her life? When will we as fellow humans accept the fact that no matter what people excel at, or aspire to, all have their faults.

When athletes win, it is because they are focused in every fiber of their body, and the same holds true of anyone who excels. Our focus for relatively short periods must not be on anything other than reaching our goal. A medium's goal should be the truth.

With mediumship we must learn to set aside our own personal feelings. This not only allows spirits to get their information and message across, but also helps to protect us from having conflicting thoughts. Those that we hold to be true and those that spirits are trying to tell us are true. One of the greatest examples of selflessness is that provided by the man known as Jesus, during his life and since. I often ask people, especially those who claim to be "very religious," what it is exactly that they see when they view the cross. It has been my experience that the more "religious" a person purports to be, the more likely the answer is to be something such as "an instrument of suffering or torture." When I look at the cross I see the letter "I" crossed out. I see that the man named Jesus, who did indeed come to "show us the way," was trying to show us that we should not put our own interests first.

One example given to me was that if a medium had strong views, say in favor of capital punishment, such a person would not make the best instrument for Spirit to use as a medium. The medium's own strong convictions could well interfere with the message of how a passed loved one who had been murdered reacted to the crime against him or her—the medium's beliefs might lead him or her to say that someone is looking for revenge. Also the medium might well influence, adversely, the spiritual message that no matter what, all life is sacred. Unless a medium can put aside his or her own feelings, for the duration of the sitting the medium is not going to be able to deliver the true word of Spirit.

It is a major fault with humans that we tend to put others on a pedestal, and although it is correct to encourage another's efforts—indeed, we can even admire those who strive to reach new heights of understanding and excellence and be encouraged by their example—the moment we place another human being on a higher pedestal than we believe ourselves to be worthy of, we are in for a bitter disappointment. If we feel that one country or political or religious leader has more rights than any other, we eventually are in for a shock, for all should be equal.

As Ramadahn succinctly answered while I was in meditation one day, "We know of no rights of nations or belief systems superior to the rights of humanity."

There have been many meditations written by truly gifted and inspired individuals for all sorts of purposes. The following is one that I have tested with groups around the world; its simplicity is the hallmark of being truly inspired. Many people, on first hearing of it, feel that it is also simple to do, but to do it well and honestly takes practice.

I suggest you read the first of the following three instructions, practice that instruction before reading and practicing the second, and then go on to the third. There is no point in running ahead and reading all three and trying to make things happen. The beauty of this is that we should not know what is going to be asked of us next, but see if we can follow what is required of us, to truly make ourselves empty vessels for Spirit to fill.

As with all meditations, it is important to sit in a way that you feel comfortable. Unless you have much practice, there is no point in trying to contort yourself into unfamiliar positions just to look the part. A solid chair with arms to rest on works just as well. Close your eyes; try to minimize any interruptions. Take a few minutes to allow yourself to be aware of your breathing.

One. Picture yourself alone in a beautiful room. You have no particular plans, but you feel as though you wish to indulge yourself. In the middle of the room there is a shaft of light. This light is of your favorite color. As you approach your favorite color you realize that the light is, in fact, made of your favorite material, whatever your fantasy material is. There is a whole bolt of it right there in the middle of the room and it is in your favorite color. As indulgent as it seems, you know you are quite alone, and you decide to drape yourself in this material, for you know how good you look in it. Also note how good it makes you feel. Use this material to fashion any garment that you choose, one in which you *know* you feel and look your best. Hold this vision for a few moments and slowly, very slowly, let the vision disappear. On opening your eyes, have a paper and pen to hand and write down everything you felt during the visualization. Be honest with yourself even if you felt guilty or extravagant.

Two. Once you have really taken in all the wonderful effects of indulging yourself, I ask you to think of a person, perhaps someone you have met, perhaps someone who annoyed or upset you, maybe a store worker who was rude or inattentive to you, someone who perhaps you were a little testy with. I ask you to visualize that person and with your mind invite that person to the same experience that you just created for yourself. It may take a little mental persuasion on your part, but if you can mentally assure that person that you mean him or her only good things, the person will allow you to give him or her that experience. You be the observer and see how the person appreciates your thoughtfulness. After a few moments let the vision go and, on opening your eyes, write down all that you witnessed.

Three. Now comes the difficult part. With the same mental vision, I want you to think of someone you dislike, if possible someone you hate, perhaps someone who was really mean to you or even hurt you. If you really have no such person in your life, think of a world figure whom you positively loathe. I ask you to invite that person to experience the same color and material that you were so willing to luxuriate in yourself. Yes, it will take an effort; yes, in your mind that person may well question your motives. However long it takes, no matter how many times you have to revisit this vision, even if you have to stop and go back to the exercise next week, even if it takes you weeks, persevere with trying to get your erstwhile enemy to have the same experience you were so willing to reward yourself with. When you do succeed with this part you will know the feeling of being an empty vessel, for you will have sought for others what you desire for yourself. This is an excellent meditation not only for mediums but also for anyone who needs to let go of past emotional pain.

GUIDES AND HELPERS

Some people are content to consult a medium and be told that they have this or that spirit guide or helper, but I have never understood why anyone would accept the word of anyone other than the spirit entities themselves. After all, these are supposedly the people who are trying to guide your life journey, so surely the person who should really get to know them is *you*!

Imagine if you went to a medium and the medium told you that you had some Egyptian priest as a guide. You could spend years believing this. I have even seen people spend a good part of their lives devoting themselves to the belief that they have some famous or well-known person as their personal guide. The facts as I have found them are these. Guides are usually spiritually advanced beings. They care little for being recognized for past efforts, and many do not even care what we call them. When the name Ramadahn was first mentioned to me, I spent many hours trying to find out if that indeed was my guide's name. All I ever got by way of explanation was, "If that is what you wish to call me, fine, but it is better that you know when I am around by your being able to sense or feel me. This is better than any label you may wish to give me."

Our guides are personal to us. We all have one primary guide, that spirit entity who holds the copy of the "shopping list" that we each write for ourselves before our birth. This is a list of spiritual lessons that we are here to learn. It is not a list that says "at twenty I will do this or at forty I will do that"; rather, it is a list of requirements that the real us has decided we need to experience or learn to further our spiritual growth. It is sad to tell that over the years I have sat through a number of meetings where the "mediums" have stated that some ancient pharaoh or Cleopatra was their guide. As with people who claim that they were royalty or famous in their past lives, my stock answer is, "If everyone was a king or queen, who built those pyramids?"

The same goes for all the Sitting Bulls and Crazy Horses, the Qwang Yings and every religious leader throughout time. The reality is that your guide is probably a humble spirit who seeks no recognition and only wants what is right for you. This criterion does not require an illumined world figure, so let's be honest with ourselves and Spirit and try not to let our imaginations run riot.

Along with the master guide there are guide helpers. These are "experts" in their fields, and in my experience these are the ones that most mediums discern when they tell you that you have an Indian guide, or a nun, or whatever. The reason the mediums discern them so readily is that these guide helpers are working very closely with you on whatever current lesson you are going through. For example, I have often said to people, "I see a nun with you." I'll go on to explain that to me a nun means patience, compassion, and tolerance. It could be that these are the virtues that the person is currently learning. The guide helpers are under the direct supervision of the master guide, and you can have more than one guide helper. This explains the confusion that sometimes occurs when one medium tells you about one guide and another detects others.

It is most important that potential mediums become acquainted with their master guide, and it is desirable that they be aware of the guide helpers. To connect with your guide and guide helpers, here is a good meditation that I use that has proved beneficial to students around the world. Sitting quietly again, really prepare yourself by trying to do everything in your power to limit any interruptions. This is, after all, about *you* and your development, so it should be important enough for you to want to exclude everything for the twenty or so minutes this will take.

Place some item of focus in front of you—a crystal, a vase of flowers, something that you can look at and see the beauty in. In the case of flowers, see the color of the petals and look at their green stems. Place them about two to three feet in front of you, and as you close your eyes try to see the flowers as buds, and with your mind's eye, see the petals slowly open and bloom. In the case of crystals, try to see deeper into the stones. Close your eyes, breathing gently in through the nose, and exhale through the mouth. Now in your mind's eye, try to "step back" from your body, if possible, to that point where you can see your physical self sitting in the chair staring at the object in front of you. Now is the time to concentrate on the heart chakra: This is where your spirit guide will most likely be seen or felt. The feeling can be at first quite emotional—after all, this is someone who has been there for you since before you came to the Earth plane. It is your acknowledgment that the trust they placed in you was well-founded. I do not expect people to get a clear picture of their guide the first time, but it is important to remember the feelings that you experience. This will help you in future attempts to decide whether you are linking with your guide or your imagination has taken over. In time and with practice you will instantly know when the guide is close. It is certainly possible for you to get to know your guide and helpers. One of the first things is to ask questions and wait for the answers. The first question I encourage everyone to ask is, "What can I do to make myself a better instrument for Spirit to use?" Always wait for an answer before moving forward with your development. Once you have connected with the guide and helpers, you will never mistake them for anyone else, for the sheer love they exude is that of a patient parent for an inquisitive child.

The following is my own observation of what the guides and helpers represent. It is in no way meant to be a definitive list, but over the years I have found that this understanding of their mission has been consistent. There is the natural law of like attracts like, and I have listed the soul group of each guide type in an effort to indicate that once you have linked with your guide you may have some idea about your own soul group. I have also listed the helper's mission so that again you may find your current lessons by learning about your helpers. There are four main soul groups—healers, teachers, philosophers, and warriors—and some 120 subgroups.

GUIDES	SOUL GROUP
Chinese/ Tibetan/ Asian Indians: Enlightenment and Understanding	Healers or Teachers
Japanese/American Indian/Indigenous Tribes: Balance and Harmony	Warriors or Healers

Appendix

Middle Eastern (includes Jews and Arabs): Justice and Peace	Philosophers or Healers
European (North): Learning and Original Ideas	Teachers or Philosophers Some Healers
All Other Nationalities: Love and Peace	Teachers, Philosophers, Healers, and Warriors

As we can see, in every example there is the possibility of being a healer, if only we take the initiative to love one another instead of hating.

Many people believe that a relative they have known who has passed becomes their guide or helper, but while this may be a comforting thought, most people we have known are not sufficiently spiritually developed to assist us. Despite this, it is certainly true that our loved ones sometimes act as go-betweens for us and the spirit helpers. After all, you are more likely to trust an uncle or grandparent whom you have known than some entity you have never met. This is our loved ones' way of helping us until we can trust our helpers. I have found that it takes practice, but after a while it is fairly easy to discern what soul group someone belongs to. When I see healers, they usually recognize themselves as people who find it hard to say no to others. They usually are good-natured, and sometimes being a little too soft with others can mean that they end up carrying other people's problems.

I always see rocks and mountains behind teachers, on the other hand. They invariably have difficult lives right from an early age. It is as if teachers have to "learn a lot" so that they can show others what can be dealt with. When I think of the warriors I immediately think of Jane Fonda, always on the front line. If there is nothing to campaign about, the likes of Ms. Fonda will find something. The philosophers are quite rare, they are highly individual. Their original thoughts can, literally, change man's way of thinking. But on the downside, they can sometimes be poor communicators. We have all heard of people who are considered brilliant, but when we speak with them, often what they have to say will go over our heads.

For the benefit of those who are interested in what role the helpers play, here is what I found to be true. Again, the list is not definitive, but it has certainly helped me to explain why some have the lessons they do have.

Spirit Helper	Lessons Being Taught
Nun or Religious Helper	Compassion, Tolerance, and Patience
American Indian/ Indigenous Tribe	Balance and Harmony

| Young Child | Trust, Honesty |
| Tibetan and Asian | Spiritual Truths |

There are of course many kinds of spirit helpers, and it is really part of the individual's development for each to discover his or her own lessons.

CHAKRAS

Chakras or psychic centers are those points in the etheric body that act as a vortex for the energy that a medium needs to work. There are many minor chakras, but the seven principal chakras are located approximately at the following locations on the body. Each has a purpose but none work independently.

1. Base of the spine. Entrance of all life force. Color is red.
2. Region just around the navel or belly button. Intuition and "gut feelings." Color is orange.
3 Spleen. Acts as a filter for "raw feelings." Color is yellow.
4. Heart. Healing. Color is green.
5. Base of the throat. This center surprises most people when they find out that it is the center for clairaudience. Hearing spirit. Color is blue.

6. Located between the eyebrows. The most well-known center, sometimes called the third eye. The color is indigo.
7. The crown chakra. The spiritual equivalent of the base center, the entrance of all spiritual knowledge. The color is violet.

There are excellent books for those seeking an in-depth understanding of the mechanics of mediumship.

One of the first things to acknowledge is that we should not try to run before we can walk. This applies to psychic as well as physical development. It is a good idea to be disciplined and set aside certain times for your advancement. If sitting alone, try it for just twenty minutes or half an hour one day a week to begin with. There is a temptation to sit in meditation for too long and far too often in the belief that more is better and that we get quicker results that way. This is not true. You will only advance at the rate that you can show you are worthy of. Also, the discipline involved in making a certain time on a set day of the week is a clear sign from you to your guides that you are serious in your endeavor.

If you feel so inclined, say a small prayer for guidance and invite your guide or helpers to draw near and make themselves known in a way that you will recognize. Next you have to open those chakras or psychic centers. Visualize a candle or a padlock, perhaps a flower bud or some image that is easy to imagine, and see this symbol at every one of your seven principal chakras. Direct your mind to the base center, and however you have thought of your symbol, see it begin to open to your mind's command. Know that these centers are linked and that as you breathe in you draw up the energy from one to the next. You may feel certain sensations as you open these centers. It is not uncommon to feel a "knot" in the solar plexus, an awareness of the heartbeat, sometimes the need to swallow as the throat center is opened. At the sixth center, or third eye, one can often sense the feeling of a band loosely tightening around the forehead. When you have opened all seven centers in this way, imagine a white light entering the crown chakra and completely flooding your whole body. See it eventually reaching your hands and feet and leaving your toes and fingers as a gray mist. Once this is done, imagine a golden liquid light entering the crown chakra, completely filling your whole body. You are now ready to begin experiencing spirit awareness.

One of the first sensations that people sometimes feel after connecting with spirit is a sense of cobwebs or a slight feeling of wisps of hair across their face. All of these sensations are just confirmation that your psychic centers are open and that they are working. These sensations can be very subtle, so do not worry if you do not perceive them at your first attempt.

In the first few attempts it is enough just to focus on opening and closing the centers. It is also important that after each session we do close these centers. To do so, start at the third eye. Let the power or energy fall away and close the centers one at a time. When you get to the base center, know that this center and the crown chakra are never fully closed, not while we are alive in the physical body. The mere act of desiring them to relax will deactivate these two centers, and after you have visualized a white light entering the crown center, use it to wash away all sensations, vibrations, and emanations. One last time, draw down a vibrant golden light and fill your very being with renewed energy, then gently visualize a small covering over that crown center. You are now closed until you wish to open again.

PSYCHOMETRY

This is a good beginner's psychic exercise, as it does not necessitate any spirit contact. The psychic centers that you use will be the solar plexus, the spleen, and the heart. These three centers are known as the collective emotional centers. They allow us to get impressions, feelings, and sensations. We cannot get visions or sound with these. Many people want to rush ahead and develop clairvoyance, to see Spirit. I can only say that your clairvoyant information will be many times enhanced if you take the time to encourage the development of these lower three centers. You should hold an item that belongs to someone else. It is helpful at this stage if you do not know the owner's identity. Just hold the item and try to feel the person. Write down or record any feelings. Clearly, you need to be able to contact the owner so that you can verify your feelings. This is a great energy exercise and a great booster of confidence when done well. Variations on this are placing items in envelopes so that you are not actually touching them. This should be attempted only after you have become proficient at reading articles that you are actually touching. Another way of doing this is to record all your feelings and sensation. Write them down, hand the owner the list of "impressions," then get the owner to answer honestly what you have correct and what you got wrong. All psychics, tarot card readers, crystal ball gazers, intuitives, and those who read runes or tea leaves use these three lower centers, whether they realize it or not. A medium uses these plus the throat and the third-eye chakra. In fact, when a medium is working well he or she is using all seven chakras.

MEDITATION

Meditation is essential for the development of mediumistic abilities. We need to enter that quietness to draw near to those who work with us. Most mediums working today will have their own routine for meditation. There are many books on this subject, but for mediums the essential part of meditation is that it be undisturbed and that it have a purpose. Many people tell me that they have sat for ages in "meditation" and received nothing. I often wonder if our guides sometimes see us sitting there with our blank minds and wonder what on Earth it is that we want. Ask a question, let your meditation have a meaning. Choose one meaningful question and meditate on that question until you get an answer. I am sure many people start meditating and ask thousands of questions. They probably get all the answers, but which answer fits which question?

Let your meditations have a purpose and enjoy them. Make sure that they are simple in their visualization. Why give yourself a difficult image that may distract you from obtaining the answers you are seeking? When I broke my leg in 1995, I remember trying to cheer myself up by thinking, "Oh, good, at least I will have more time for meditation, maybe I will be able to move ahead." Ramadahn quickly told me, "Keep the pace you are going at; it is quality not quantity that we need." He also added a rather witty, "Besides, where do you think you are running to?"

INSPIRATION

A good test for inspiration is to think of a subject, perhaps one you know well, and sit as for meditation. Open all the centers, but especially direct the energy to the heart. Let us for argument's sake say you chose the subject of love. Reflect on this word and what it means to you and see the energy especially going to the heart and the crown chakra. If you get any words, thoughts, or impressions that seem to be of just a slightly higher knowledge or understanding than your own, make a note of them. If any of the information helps you to see any subject in a different or even more positive way than you have before, then it is likely that someone is trying to inspire you.

CLAIRVOYANCE

To practice clairvoyance, draw the energy to the center in the middle of the forehead. Do not strain or try to rush anything, and be content if in the first attempts you only see swirling lights or even colors. True clairvoyance takes a lot of practice and it is rarely developed while we are sitting alone. The best place for the effective development of clairvoyance is in a circle with an experienced teacher. The same goes for clairaudience, except that with this gift we need to direct the energy to the throat center.

Although there is much that you can do to prepare yourself for mediumship development, I really feel that there is no substitute for a good, experienced teacher and a harmonious circle of like-minded people.

I hope this book has encouraged you in your quest for an answer to man's oldest question.

TWO SITTINGS
WITH ROBERT BROWN

My name is Bill and I live in Lutz, Florida. My initial experience with Robert Brown was in a telephone session in July 1998. I had never before consulted a medium. In fact, I had never even given much thought or credibility to mediums prior to this session with Robert. But I was driven by desperation to know if my loved one on the other side was okay, and I also needed a confirmation from my loved one in the spiritual plane that he was still with me here in the physical world.

Going into that first telephone session with Robert, I honestly did not know what to expect. I halfway doubted anything meaningful would come out of the phone session. I somewhat felt it would be like going to a fortune teller at a carnival, and that all I would get from the session would be generic statements and suggestions. Of course I was also hoping for more than that—and I received it.

I was hoping to reach my son who had been the victim of a brutal homicide in November 1997. He had been beaten by several young street punks who kicked, punched, and beat him with baseball bats. They did not even know him. It was a senseless killing just for the sheer pleasure of beating someone who was in a helpless situation. My son was pleading for them to stop hitting him and screaming for help but they did not stop beating him. They laughed and cursed him while they continued to beat him. I can still picture him on that cold concrete, totally helpless and alone and being beaten. He was on life support for three days and then the hospital told us our son was brain dead. I argued with the doctors, told them there must be more that could be done; I made them show me the X rays of his brain. But in the end it was true, my son, my pride and joy, was never coming home again. We turned the life support system off at 7:30 P.M. on November 19, 1997. My wife and I stood by him, holding his hand and crying. His heart was strong. It beat for fifteen minutes, gradually slowing down until it finally stopped. He was twenty-one years old and he was gone.

The void so cruelly created in my world as a result of my son's death cannot be put into words. It totally consumed me. This boy was to start working in my business in a few weeks. I had just bought a truck for him to use in the business. Just a matter of hours earlier on the day of his beating we had spoken on the telephone and we had made plans for him to come over to our home the next Monday evening so that we could watch the Monday Night Football game together.

Robert knew none of the preceding when we had our first telephone session. Yet, within a few minutes Robert was able to confirm to me the manner in which my son died and that he had died before his time, that he was a young person. Robert was also able to discern the number of people who beat him that cold November night. He went on to describe to me a collage of pictures of my son that I had assembled in my office after his death. Additionally, Robert was able to discern that this collage of photos was on top of another large picture in the frame and to confirm that fact, Robert gave me a list of names that were imprinted on that picture, under the collage of photos I had put together. When I checked later, after the phone session, I was able to locate five of the seven names Robert had given to me. Again, Robert had never spoken to me before and he certainly was never in my home. This was a confirmation to me that Robert was getting his information from my son.

Robert then went on to describe my son and his characteristics such as his cheerful, helpful nature throughout his short life. Robert was able to describe my son's physical attributes including his haircut style and the fact that earlier on the night my son was beaten, he was having his hair cut. This was true. Just a couple hours before he was beaten my son did have his hair cut in his apartment by one of his friends. Robert then went on to state that someone had gone to my son's apartment after his death looking for a locket of his hair. I did not recall that at the time of the session but on reflection later, after the session I did remember that when my wife and I went to my son's apartment to clean up after his death, I did go into the bathroom and glanced into the sink looking for some of my son's hair. Robert told me that he saw someone reading something at my son's funeral and then folding it up and putting it away in a pocket. In fact, at my son's funeral I did read a memorial statement and after I read it, I did in fact fold it up and put it into my coat pocket.

My impression after that first session was phenomenal. Robert was able to tell me so many things that he had no prior knowledge of or about. I wanted more! I wanted to see if Robert could do as well in another phone session—that would be the proof. My second telephone session with Robert was in May 1999. And I went into that session hoping it would be as fruitful as the first and, again, Robert did not disappoint me. Robert linked with my son and told me about a dream about my son that I had recently had that was also correct. Robert then asked me if my son had damaged his head at all and I replied, "Yes." Robert then went on to confirm to me that my son had helped my mother-in-law when she passed over, he was waiting there for her. My son relayed to Robert that he was "knocked out of this world," and that it was "no accident." My son then went on to tell Robert that he liked his "altar." Which is in fact a table on which I have his photograph and where I frequently talk to him. His picture sits directly under a table lamp that illuminates his face when the lamp is on. Here again, this is something that Robert would have no knowledge of, having never been to my home. Amazingly, Robert indicated to me that my son was calling up the date October 18 and indicating something would happen on that upcoming date. At the time of this session in May, the date October 18 had no meaning for me. As it later turned out, October 18 was the date we settled our litigation action against the apartment complex where my son was living at the time he was beaten. This was a prediction relayed by Robert, from my son in the spirit world. There was one more telephone session with Robert during which Robert was again able to link with my son in the spirit world and relay to me very personal and specific messages from my loved one that could only have come from the other side.

I have gotten a sense of reassurance, consolation, peace, and hope from my sessions with Robert Brown. While I still miss my son and I can to some extent communicate with him in my mind, it is so much clearer when I have a session with Robert and I can actually ask questions of my son and get an immediate answer. As has happened in a couple of our sessions, sometimes my son's answers do not make sense to Robert at all. That, in my mind is even more confirmation that Robert is truly linking with my son in the spirit world.

There are many people and even some religions that do not approve of mediums; the Catholic Church for one considers mediums to be Satan's helpers. I do not understand that. Robert has never done or said anything that would be considered antireligion. He has always imparted only words of peace, consolation, and love.

I feel very lucky to have found Robert Brown as a source to communicate with my loved one in the spirit world. He has made a true believer out of me and I look forward to many more sessions with him.

❋

The first time I met Robert Brown was in May of 2000 while attending a fabulous retreat in Barbados with three other well-known mediums and two other gifted teachers. The purpose of the retreat was to learn how to access our own abilities in psychic mediumship and to experience the once in a lifetime opportunity of participation in a series of small group readings with each of these incredible mediums. My mother and I were assigned to a small group and all of us stayed together throughout the rotation of the four mediums.

Our first group reading was with Robert. My mother and I were excited, apprehensive, and skeptical as well. I was extremely emotional during that sitting because of how my maternal grandmother came through. Robert's physical description of her mannerisms, personality, sense of humor, and the illnesses, which she endured prior to her passing, were so accurate that I experienced a visceral reaction. My heart felt like it was in my throat and the tears streamed down my face for the entire reading. It felt as though Nana was standing right there with us. However, some of the information Robert conveyed from my grandmother about how I had needed to be "very strong" at that time and how "the rug had been pulled out from under me" over the last six months gave me pause. I could not validate some of those details initially. It wasn't until much later that I realized we weren't experiencing "psychic amnesia," but, in fact, a prediction.

Our trip to Barbados was one of those life-changing spiritual experiences you sometimes hear people describe. The basic skills we learned during the retreat regarding techniques for relaxation, opening up, meditation, and psychic development sparked my already avid interest. So, it was a natural progression for me to continue pursuing this area when Robert offered another workshop on psychic development this past October. My sister and I attended. During an exercise, Robert was assisting one participant in reading another person who happened to be sitting two rows directly in front of my sister and I when a few very specific pieces of information came through that could not be validated by that young woman, but most definitely applied to us. My sister's birthday, my mother's name, and a piece of jewelry my maternal grandmother was known for. We kept whispering to each other, "It's Nana!" However, we didn't want to intrude. Shortly after this workshop, we decided Nana was trying to come through with a message and we inquired about a private sitting with Robert. It didn't surprise us that Nana had come through to us in this way, as she was extremely vocal and humorous in life and apparently on the other side as well. As always, when things are meant to be, they occur. Pam, Robert's assistant, fit us into his schedule where there had been a cancellation. We were thrilled, but a little nervous.

In the interim, between the workshop and the reading, many events had unfolded. My parents had returned from a vacation in Europe, which was less than pleasant due to the fact that my mother began mani-festing symptoms of a serious illness. The morning of the scheduled reading, we had taken her to the doctor and they had done some testing for cancer. Now the statements Robert had mentioned in Barbados six months before about how "the rug had been pulled out from under me" and having "to be very strong" made perfect sense to me. I was grateful that my grandmother was persistent in her efforts to get messages through to us during Robert's workshop and that we now had that appointment which we desperately needed.

On November 10th, during that private sitting, our maternal grandmother did indeed come through with powerful messages about our mom and her ill-ness. Nana's message provided a lot of hope saying, "They're not ready for her yet," when Robert asked if my grandmother was expecting Mom on the other side. Robert stated he saw this whole thing as a "wakeup call" but Mom would have to go through some things here on the physical side before it was resolved. This provided us with a tremendous amount of relief. Thankfully, as I am writing this, Mom has just com-pleted her treatments and is on the road to recovery.

Our paternal grandfather came through as well and Robert very accurately described his physical appear-ance, personality, and demeanor while he was still alive. Grandpa provided us with messages of strength and information about our spiritual development over the last few years which was accurate as well.

Then my brother came through, whom Robert called the "principal person." Robert described him as someone with a "very good smile" and saw him in "spirit clothes." He added that he appeared almost ephemeral and looked like a "fresh-faced friendly priest." Robert said he never sees spirit clothes unless they mean something and felt my brother had attained a higher level, but my brother didn't want him to elevate his status. Interestingly enough, this was how my mother and I had envisioned my brother during previous meditations in Barbados in which the mediums guided us to connect with our loved ones. Another connection could be one my daughter just pointed out: the accident which caused his passing happened on the front lawn of a church.

Due to the fact that my brother was in a coma prior to his passing, Robert felt he could ask him some questions such as "What is the point of death?" My brother conveyed that although his body lingered physically, he had already passed on and had observed everything that was happening. Robert asked him to prove that. It was then that my brother described an event with Robert's assistance, where he stated he was next to a machine that had a flat line on the monitor or one that was just barely registering. This was truly accurate as my brother was diagnosed with only about 1 percent of his brain functioning. Robert asked if he was in any pain and he said, the only pain he felt was watching us go through our own grief and grasp at hope . . . but now we really do have hope.

My brother also related information about an event that happened prior to his death of which my sister and I had no knowledge. He described five people standing around the bed praying. After our reading, we asked my mother about it and received confirmation from her.

Throughout the reading, there were lights flickering and sounds manifesting in the room, which we all laughed about. We had experienced phenomena like this before when we had felt the presence of our deceased relatives. Robert asked my brother another question that is frequently asked of him, "Are those who have passed on always around?" My brother's answer was, "Sometimes nearer . . . sometimes farther." At that point, a noise came from the general direction where Robert had previously stated he saw my brother standing. It startled us, and my sister said jokingly, "He is here now!" We all burst into laughter. Information that brought me comfort was when my brother stated "they" are always around when there is a need. "They" go to those who need it most. He also said "they" can be around more than one person at a time. Robert stated that my brother was around my mom and dad most at that time, as they were quite shaken up about my mother's illness.

A great deal of information was provided during that sitting; it is difficult to recount it all. Other facts about interpersonal relationships with family members who are still living were conveyed as well. On both occasions, when I have had the sittings with Robert, I came away feeling astonished, not only at the amount of information provided, but its accuracy. I used to be afraid of this whole process and was very skeptical. Now I strongly recommend it to people who are grieving over the death of their loved ones, due to the comfort it brought me.

This reading had a profound effect on all of us. Hearing those messages of hope from deceased relatives provided us with the strength and determination to do whatever we needed to help our mom and dad through this health crisis. When we shared our reading with Mom, I'll never forget that look of amazement and relief on her face. With a small smile, Mom shared with us the special message Nana had sent to her: "They're not ready for you yet" was the phrase my mother told Nana on many occasions before my grandmother passed. I firmly believe hearing my grandmother pass along a message using that very same phrase, in the midst of her fight against cancer, helped Mom get through a very difficult process and gave her some peace of mind. The whole sitting was a godsend for my family. It reaffirmed what we had always felt in our hearts, our family on the other side was still loving and supporting us.

Contact address and Web site:
Robert Brown
P.O. Box 646
Merrick, NY 11566-0646
Web site www.robertbrown-medium.com

Web sites that may be of help and interest:
ADC
  www.after-death.com
The Learning Light Foundation
  www.learninglight.org
International Spiritualist Federation
  www.internationalspirit.mcmail.com
Center for Human Development
  www.espcenter.com
Leslie Flint Education Trust
  www.leslieflint.com
The Compassionate Friends
  www.compassionatefriends.org